T0316582

Cambridge Elements ≡

Elements in Ethics
edited by
Ben Eggleston
University of Kansas
Dale E. Miller
Old Dominion University, Virginia

MORALITY AND PRACTICAL REASONS

Douglas W. Portmore
Arizona State University

CAMBRIDGE
UNIVERSITY PRESS

CAMBRIDGE
UNIVERSITY PRESS

University Printing House, Cambridge CB2 8BS, United Kingdom

One Liberty Plaza, 20th Floor, New York, NY 10006, USA

477 Williamstown Road, Port Melbourne, VIC 3207, Australia

314–321, 3rd Floor, Plot 3, Splendor Forum, Jasola District Centre, New Delhi – 110025, India

79 Anson Road, #06–04/06, Singapore 079906

Cambridge University Press is part of the University of Cambridge.

It furthers the University's mission by disseminating knowledge in the pursuit of education, learning, and research at the highest international levels of excellence.

www.cambridge.org
Information on this title: www.cambridge.org/9781108706384
DOI: 10.1017/9781108580724

© Douglas W. Portmore 2021

First published 2021

A catalogue record for this publication is available from the British Library.

ISBN 978-1-108-70638-4 Paperback
ISSN 2516-4031 (online)
ISSN 2516-4023 (print)

Morality and Practical Reasons

Elements in Ethics

DOI: 10.1017/9781108580724
First published online: February 2021

Douglas W. Portmore
Arizona State University

Author for correspondence: Douglas W. Portmore, dwportmore@gmail.com

Abstract: As Socrates famously noted, there is no more important question than how we ought to live. The answer to this question depends on how the reasons that we have for living in various different ways combine and compete. To illustrate, suppose that I've just received a substantial raise. What should I do with the extra money? I have most moral reason to donate it to effective charities but most self-interested reason to spend it on luxuries for myself. So, whether I should live my life as I have most moral reason to live it or as I have most self-interested reason to live it depends on how these and other sorts of reasons combine and compete to determine what I have most reason to do, all things considered. This Element seeks to figure out how different sorts of reasons combine and compete to determine how we ought to live.

Keywords: morality, rationality, reasons, normativity, self-interest

Isbns: 9781108706384 (PB), 9781108580724 (OC)
Issns: 2516–4031 (online), 2516–4023 (print)

Contents

1 Morality and How We Ought to Live

Whereas primitive animals are ruled by their impulses, we humans are rational creatures who can respond to reasons for acting contrary to our impulses. We are therefore capable of directing our lives in accordance with our reasons rather than just being swept along by the flow of our impulses. So it's important for us to ask how we ought to live, as the answer to this question will tell us what living in accordance with our reasons entails. After all, how we ought to live just depends on how our various practical reasons – our reasons for living in different ways – combine and compete to determine *the* way (or, if there's a tie for first place, *the ways*) that we have most reason to live, all things considered. The relevant reasons are practical reasons. And *practical* reasons differ from other types of reasons in that they count for or against *performing (or intending to perform) certain actions*, whereas other types of reasons count for or against having some other kind of response. For instance, *epistemic* reasons typically count for or against *believing certain propositions*. And *evaluative* reasons typically count for or against *desiring certain states of affairs*. Now, I'll be concerned almost exclusively with practical reasons. So the reader should assume that, unless I explicitly state otherwise, the reasons that I'm discussing are practical reasons.

As just suggested, there seem to be different sorts of (practical) reasons. For instance, whereas the balance of moral reasons supports doing what's most morally choiceworthy, the balance of self-interested reasons supports doing what's most self-interestedly choiceworthy. But how do these different sorts of reasons combine and compete to determine which is most choiceworthy overall? And which is the way that we ought to live? Should we live as it would be most morally choiceworthy to live, as it would be most self-interestedly choiceworthy to live, or as it would be most overall choiceworthy to live? The question arises because these can seemingly come apart. After all, the most morally choiceworthy way to live may not be the most overall choiceworthy way to live. Consider that those known as *effective altruists* believe that the most morally choiceworthy way for you to live is by maximizing the good that you do over the course of your life.[1] Some of them even go so far as to suggest that you ought to earn as much as possible with the goal of giving most of what you earn (say, everything over the $35,000 a year that you need to subsist) to effective charities. And they argue that it would be better for you to work on Wall Street and earn lots of extra money that you then give away to charity than to work in a profession in which you help people directly but make very little extra money that you can then donate to charity. They argue that, as a nurse, teacher, or social worker, you would make the world better only by the margin

---

[1] Two prominent effective altruists are William MacAskill (2015) and Peter Singer (2015).

that you do that job better than whoever would have otherwise done it. But as an effective altruist working on Wall Street, you can make much more of a difference because the person who would have otherwise filled your position would almost certainly have used the substantial extra earnings that you'll give to charity on luxuries for herself – and so you'll do much more good with those extra earnings than she would have.[2]

So, according to many effective altruists, the most morally choiceworthy life for a young person is the one in which they work to become an investment banker on Wall Street and then donate all but what they need for bare subsistence to the most effective charities that they can find. Such a person won't be able to afford to raise a family, for it isn't easy living in New York City on only $35,000 a year. And they'll almost certainly need to live in a cramped apartment with several roommates just to afford the high rents in that city. What's more, they'll need to forgo expensive hobbies, such as golfing, scuba diving, music lessons, and art collecting. Last, they'll need to forgo the luxuries that many of us take for granted: vacations, dinners out, streaming services, nights at the theatre, etc. Indeed, when they get some time off work, they should probably use it to recover from a surgery in which they have donated one of their kidneys to a stranger in renal failure. For, as some effective altruists have argued, the risk of dying as a result of making such a donation is only one in four thousand and so to refrain from making such a donation would be to value their own life four thousand times more than that of the stranger.[3]

But even if living in the single-minded pursuit of doing the most good that one can is perhaps the most morally choiceworthy way to live, it may not be the most overall choiceworthy way to live. After all, it seems that we have good reason to pursue more well-rounded lives – see, for example, Berg (Manuscript). It seems, for instance, that I have good reason to live a life in which I raise a family, travel the world, attend the theatre, take music lessons, and pursue a career that I find more rewarding than any on Wall Street. Thus it seems that even if I could do more good by plugging away as an investment banker on Wall Street and donating most of what I earn to effective charities, I have good reason to want to interact face-to-face with the people whom I'm helping (e.g., my students) while doing the kind of work that I find fulfilling (e.g., teaching).

Of course all of this has been rather quick. I've just assumed that the effective altruist is correct about its being most morally choiceworthy to maximize the good that one does. And I've just assumed that the reasons that one has, say, to take a vacation or pursue a fulfilling career are nonmoral reasons, and that these

---

[2] See, for instance, MacAskill (2013).   [3] For some examples, see Baggini (2015).

nonmoral reasons are not outweighed, overridden, or undermined by the moral reasons that one has instead to do as much good as possible. Yet it does seem that the most morally choiceworthy life is just the life that one has most moral reason to live. And it seems that the most overall choiceworthy life is just the life that one has most reason to live, all things (including both moral and nonmoral reasons) considered. So it seems that, in order to determine both what's most morally choiceworthy and what's most choiceworthy overall, we need to better understand what our reasons are, which of them are moral, which of them are nonmoral, and how they combine and compete to determine what we have most reason to do, all things considered. And this is what I aim to do, starting with an exploration of the nature of moral reasons.

2 The Nature of Moral Reasons

Moral reasons are a subset of normative reasons. Thus, to understand them, we must first understand what *normative* reasons are and how they differ from *nonnormative* reasons, such as explanatory reasons and motivating reasons. What's more, we need to understand how moral reasons differ from other kinds of normative reasons. In particular, we need to understand how *moral* reasons differ from *nonmoral* reasons. And we need to understand how normative reasons differ from facts that are relevant to how we ought to live but that are not themselves normative reasons – that is, how they differ from what I call *normatively relevant non-reasons*. The relations among these various notions are depicted in Figure 1.

2.1 Normative Reasons versus Nonnormative Reasons

A normative reason is a fact that counts for or against a subject's responding in a certain way to their circumstances. It counts for or against this response in that it counts for or against this being how they ought to respond.[4] For instance, the fact that I'll probably need a root canal later if I don't get this cavity taken care of right away is a normative reason for me to get it taken care of right away. That is, it counts in favor of this being what I ought to do in that this will be what I ought to do unless some other fact defeats its favoring force. More precisely, then, we can define normative reasons for and against as follows.

---

[4] Others believe that there's nothing to be said beyond saying that they count in favor of some response. Here's Tim Scanlon (1998, p. 17): "Any attempt to explain what it is to be a reason for something seems to me to lead back to the same idea: a consideration that counts in favor of it. 'Counts in favor how?' one might ask. 'By providing a reason for it' seems to be the only answer." And still others agree with me that more can be said but disagree with me about what more can be said. For instance, Julia Markovits (2014, pp. 2–3) holds that "what it *is* for a consideration to count in favor of an action is for it … to help satisfy one of [the agent's] desires."

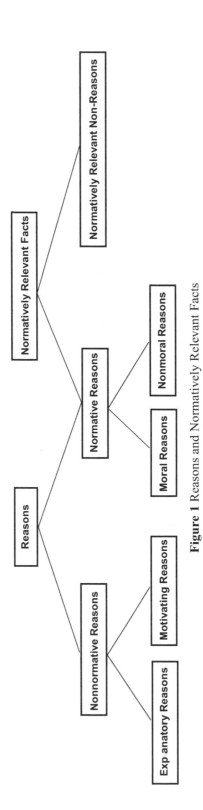

Figure 1 Reasons and Normatively Relevant Facts

Normative Reasons: For any subject S with the option of φ-ing in circumstances C, a normative reason *for* S to φ in C is any fact that will, absent its favoring force being defeated, make it the case that their φ-ing in C is what is most overall choiceworthy and, thus, what they *ought*, all things considered, to do in C.[5] And a normative reason *against* S's φ-ing in C is any fact that will, absent its disfavoring force being defeated, make it the case that they *ought not*, all things considered, to φ in C.

Given that there can be normative reasons both for and against one's φ-ing, normative reasons can conflict. The fact that I'll probably need a root canal if I don't get this cavity taken care of right away is a normative reason for me to get it taken care of right away, but the fact that I'm really pressed for time and need to finish a project at work by the end of the week is a normative reason against my doing so. Thus, whether I ought to take care of it right away depends (in part) on whether these reasons against doing so are defeated. And there are a number of possible ways that they might be. One possibility is that the reasons for getting the cavity taken care of right away *nullify* or otherwise *undermine* the disfavoring force of the reasons against doing so. To illustrate, suppose that I promised my wife that I wouldn't let work interfere with my healthcare. Perhaps this promise-related reason nullifies the work-related reason, undermining whatever disfavoring force that it would otherwise have. Another possibility is that health-related reasons always *override* work-related reasons such that even the weakest health-related reason for getting it taken care of right away trumps the strongest work-related reason against doing so. And a third possibility is that the reasons for taking care of it right away *outweigh* the reasons against doing so. For perhaps the combined favoring force of all the reasons for taking care of it right away outweighs the combined disfavoring force of all the reasons against doing so.[6]

---

[5] Jonathan Dancy has claimed that some normative reasons for φ-ing (what he calls "enticing reasons" for φ-ing) favor one's φ-ing without being such that they will, absent being defeated, make it the case that one ought to φ. He claims that "they go to make a choice the best one, but not yet the one which one ought to take" (2004, p. 116). He denies that these enticing reasons can take us to an ought, because he denies that they can take us to an obligation and believes that we're obligated to do whatever we ought to do (2006a, p. 135). Yet it seems clear both that one ought to take whatever option one has most reason to take and that one isn't always obligated to take the option that one has most reason to take – more on this later in this Element. So, contrary to Dancy, I believe that what makes a normative reason for one to φ an enticing reason, rather than a requiring reason, is that it's a fact that favors one's φ-ing without giving anyone (even oneself) sufficient grounds for demanding that one φs. It does, however, take us to an ought if undefeated.

[6] When combining the forces of reasons, we should never combine the force of a derivative reason with that of the reason from which its force derives. That would involve a kind of problematic double-counting. Thus, when I talk about combining the forces of reasons, I'm talking about combining the forces of only nonderivative reasons. See Nair (2016).

Note, then, that the favoring and disfavoring forces of normative reasons can be more or less weighty. That is, normative reasons can favor or disfavor an action to a greater or lesser degree. And the weights of these forces can combine and compete with those of other normative reasons. What's more, the combined favoring force of a multitude of relatively weak reasons for one to φ could outweigh the disfavoring force of a relatively strong reason against one's φ-ing: the result being that one ought to φ even though none of the individual reasons that one has for φ-ing could, on its own, outweigh the strong reason one has against φ-ing. To illustrate, suppose that I have a weighty reason against going into the office today: I'll lose more than an hour of productivity just in the time it would take to commute to and from the office. And suppose that I have only one student who wants to meet with me today. In that case, the relatively weak favoring force of this reason would, we'll suppose, be defeated by the comparatively strong disfavoring force of the reason that I have against going into the office. But now suppose that I have instead a total of five students who each want to meet with me today. In that case, the combined force of each of these reasons would, we'll suppose, defeat the disfavoring force of the reason that I have against going into the office. So if I have only one student who wants to meet with me, I ought not to go into the office. But if I have five students who want to meet with me, I ought to go into the office.

As we've just seen, if I have an undefeated normative reason to φ in C, then φ is what I ought to do in C. And it's this ability to combine and compete so as to determine what one ought to do that's definitive of normative reasons. Normative reasons are normative in that they can contribute both to generating oughts and to preventing other reasons from generating oughts.

It's important to note, though, that a fact that doesn't provide an agent with a normative reason to φ in one set of circumstances could provide them with a normative reason to φ in another set of circumstances. For instance, the fact that I've promised that I would go into the office if and only if I have some other reason to go into the office doesn't provide me with a reason to go into the office in those circumstances in which I don't have any other reason to go into the office, but it does provide me with a reason to go into the office in those circumstances in which, say, I have a meeting at the office that I have good reason to attend (Dancy 2006b, p. 42).

It's also important to note that normative reasons, if not defeated, necessarily take us to an *ought*, but they don't necessarily take us to an *obligation*. For although we ought to do whatever we are obligated to do, not everything that we ought to do is something that we're obligated to do. To say that an act is one that you ought to perform is to say that it's the option that you have most reason to perform, and it is therefore your most choiceworthy option.[7] But to say that an act is one that you're obligated to perform is to say additionally that you would be blameworthy for failing to perform it absent some suitable excuse.[8] Thus, an act can be one that you ought to perform without being one that you are obligated to perform. For you are not always blameworthy for failing to perform the option that you have most reason to perform – even when you lack a suitable excuse for so failing. Whether you are or not just depends on whether there is some actual or hypothetical person (either oneself or some other) who can rightfully demand that you perform this option. Thus, there has to be some (at least, possible) person who can rightfully hold you to account (by blaming you) if you fail to perform it without having some suitable excuse. To illustrate, consider the following claim: "I ought to send my mother flowers for Mother's Day, but, at the very least, I must send her a card." This claim, I take it, expresses the thought that what I have most reason to do is to send her flowers, but that I'm obligated at a minimum to send her a card. This is the least that I could do because she has every right to demand that I do at least this much given all that she's done for me. And although neither she nor anyone else has the right to demand that I send her flowers, I ought to do so given what it would mean to her and how little it would inconvenience me to do so, which is what explains why this is what I have most reason to do.

As I've just explained, normative reasons are related to oughts; they can contribute both to generating an ought and to preventing other reasons from generating an ought. It's potentially confusing, then, that in ordinary English we often use the word "reasons" to refer to things that are not related to oughts. So, to avoid confusion, we should label these reasons that are not related to oughts "nonnormative reasons."

There are at least two types of nonnormative reasons: *explanatory reasons* and *motivating reasons*. I'll consider each in turn. An explanatory reason explains why a subject responded as they did. For instance, the fact that I haven't gotten enough sleep lately may explain why I've just snapped at you

---

[7] I take all the following to be equivalent: "you ought to φ," "you have most reason to φ," and "φ is your most choiceworthy option." But I take all three to be distinct from "φ is your best option." For why, see Portmore (2019a, especially chap. 6).

[8] Note that I'm assuming that there is nonmoral blame as well as moral blame – see Portmore (Forthcoming). What distinguishes moral blame from nonmoral blame is, I believe, the different sorts of reactive attitudes that are associated with each. For instance, moral blame (unlike nonmoral blame) involves in its first-person instances feelings of guilt. And this allows us to distinguish moral oughts and obligations from nonmoral oughts and obligations. If you fail to do what you're morally obligated to do without any suitable excuse, it will be fitting for you to feel guilty. And if you fail to do what you morally ought to do without any suitable excuse, it will (or would be) fitting for you to feel guilty if there is (or had been) someone who could have rightly demand(ed) that you do as you morally ought to.

(Markovits 2014, p. 1). But of course my not having gotten enough sleep lately doesn't count in favor of my snapping at you. Rather, it's merely what caused me to snap at you. And so explanatory reasons are distinct from normative reasons – they are facts that explain why an agent did what they did without necessarily counting in favor of what they did. By contrast, a normative reason for performing an action, by conceptual necessity, counts in favor of performing that action.[9]

Another type of nonnormative reason is a motivating reason. Consider that even if I snap at you because I haven't been getting enough sleep lately, this won't be the consideration on the basis of which I chose to snap at you. Perhaps I chose to snap at you because you had been tapping your foot and this had gotten on my nerves (Markovits 2014, p. 1). But of course the consideration on the basis of which I chose to snap at you needn't be one that counts in favor of my doing so. The fact that you'd been tapping your foot doesn't count in favor of my snapping at you. Thus, motivating reasons are also distinct from normative reasons – they are the considerations on the basis of which the agent chooses to act without necessarily being considerations that count in favor of that act. And note that, unless I explicitly state otherwise, I'll use the term "reasons" to refer to normative reasons.

2.2 Qualified Normativity versus Unqualified Normativity

I've claimed that what's definitive of normative reasons is that they contribute both to generating oughts and to preventing other reasons from generating oughts. But what sorts of oughts? Interestingly, some philosophers deny that there's anything that we just plain ought to do. They claim instead that there is only what we legally ought to do, what we morally ought to do, what we self-interestedly ought to do, what we aesthetically ought to do, etc. That is, they deny that there is anything that we just plain ought to do and hold instead that there is only what we ought to do in various qualified senses. These philosophers are known as *normative pluralists*.[10] To illustrate, suppose that I'm playing chess, I'm in check, and it's my turn.[11] The rules of chess dictate that, given that I'm in check, I must move my king one square to the left – this being the only move that gets me out of check. But the rules of etiquette dictate that I ought instead to resign by tipping over my king because I can no longer expect

---

[9] Sometimes, when an agent is motivated to act by a fact that counts in favor of that act, that very fact counts not only as a motivating reason, but also as both an explanatory reason and a normative reason (Markovits 2014, p. 1).

[10] Proponents of normative pluralism include David Copp (1997, 2009), Mathias Sagdahl (2014), and Evan Tiffany (2007). Critics include Owen McLeod (2001) and Dale Dorsey (2016).

[11] This example is borrowed from Richard Joyce (2001, p. 50).

a draw, let alone a win. Yet, from the point of view of self-interest, I ought to offer a draw because I don't want to lose and my opponent doesn't yet realize how untenable my situation has become. Last, let's suppose that morality directs me to violate the rules of chess by using my cell phone during the game given that I promised my wife that I would text her during the game. In such a case, normative pluralists hold that I morally ought to use my cell phone, self-interestedly ought to offer a draw, etiquettically ought to resign, and chess-rules-wise ought to move my king one square to the left. But they deny that there's anything that I just plain ought to do – that is, they deny that there's anything that I ought to do, all things considered.

We should, I believe, be skeptical of normative pluralism. After all, when ordinary people (those without advanced training in contemporary moral philosophy) use the word "ought," they rarely, if ever, use any overt qualifier with it. That is, they rarely, if ever, use constructions such as "morally ought," "legally ought," "prudentially ought," or "self-interestedly ought."[12] And I doubt that they intend for there to be some covert qualifier attached to their "ought" that's supposedly fixed by the context. For it seems that when ordinary people use the word "ought," they use it in an unqualified way that's meant to be authoritative such that if you don't respond as they say that you ought to, they take you to be guilty of a mistake from the point of view of reasons generally and not just from the point of view of some qualified normative perspective. Thus, we wouldn't tell someone that they ought to wait for everyone else to be served before taking a bite of their food when we know that they are a diabetic with a dangerously low blood sugar level. That is, we wouldn't presume that, in the context, our statement would mean only that this is what they etiquettically ought to do even though doing so would clearly be a mistake from the point of view of reasons generally.

Of course, whenever you violate a standard – whether it be one of legality, morality, etiquette, or reasons generally – you'll be guilty of the "mistake" of having violated that standard. But, for any standard other than that of reasons generally, it's an open question whether you'll also be guilty of the mistake of not responding appropriately to your reasons. After all, you may not have any reason to abide by the given standard. For standards come cheap in that they can

---

[12] On March 17, 2020, I did a search of the online version of the *New York Times* (www.nytimes.com). And whereas I got 820,437 results for "ought," I got only two results for "legally ought," one result for "morally ought," and zero results both for "self-interestedly ought" and for "prudentially ought." The one result for "morally ought" was due to a quotation from Oxford academic Richard Dawkins. And of the two results for "legally ought," one seemed to be the result of a transcription error and the other was due to a quotation by a highly educated congressman who has both a BA and a JD from Harvard.

be constructed for any or no purpose at all.[13] Consider, for instance, what we might call *the many-books standard*: an act meets this standard if and only if it involves touching three or more distinct books.[14] Thus, the act of arranging a stack of several distinct books meets this standard, but the act of jogging around the neighborhood doesn't. Thus, in jogging around the neighbouhood, one makes the "mistake" of violating the many-books standard. But if one doesn't have any reason to abide by this standard, then one isn't making the mistake of responding inappropriately to one's reasons.

So one reason to reject normative pluralism is the fact that it conflicts with the way that ordinary English speakers tend to use the word "ought." They tend to use it in an unqualified way such that those who fail to do as they say that they ought to are taken to be guilty of having failed to respond appropriately to their reasons.[15] Indeed, few people would say that you ought to do something simply because it is in accordance with just any old standard, such as the many-books standard. For it is only some standards that we have reason to abide by. And because of this we can sensibly ask whether we just plain ought to do what we ought to do in some qualified sense – for example, whether we ought to do what we many-books-wise ought to do. So another reason to think that there is this unqualified sense of ought is the fact that we seem to be able to ask questions such as whether we ought to do what we legally, morally, or self-interestedly ought to do. And such questions presuppose that there is an unqualified sense of "ought."

Last, we should reject normative pluralism because it often seems to us that there's a normative question that needs answering even when we know what we ought to do in every qualified sense of "ought." For instance, sometimes I morally ought to do one thing but self-interestedly ought to do another. And yet it seems important to inquire further and ask what I ought to do, all things considered – that is, what I ought to do considering both what is most morally choiceworthy and what is most self-interestedly choiceworthy. And, in some

---

[13] Some normative pluralists – those who we might call *restricted* normative pluralists (e.g., Copp 2009) – hold that there are only a limited number of domains that are normative in the relevant sense – perhaps just morality and self-interest. But they hold that, because these domains are incommensurable, there is nothing that we ought to do, all things considered, but only what we ought to do in the various qualified senses. A challenge for such restricted normative pluralists is to explain what the relevant sense of "normative" is such that some but not all standards of evaluation are normative if it's not just that some but not all such standards are those that we have unqualified reasons to abide by.

[14] This is inspired by a similar example from Dale Dorsey (2016, p. 9).

[15] As I see it, failing to do what one ought to do entails failing to respond appropriately to one's reasons in that it is inappropriate for one to fail to do what one has most reason to do. But if no one (not even oneself) can legitimately demand that one does what one has most reason to do in the circumstances, then one will be neither required to do so nor blameworthy for failing to do so.

cases, it seems that I ought to do what is most morally choiceworthy, whereas, in other cases, it seems that I ought to do what is most self-interestedly choice-worthy. To illustrate, suppose that I promised to meet a student Friday afternoon to help them with their term paper. But suppose that, come Friday afternoon, I'm rather tired and would prefer to take a nap. In such a case, I morally ought to meet with them, but I self-interestedly ought to take a nap. What's more, in this case, it seems that what I ought to do, all things considered, is meet with them as promised. For it seems that when determining what I ought to do, all things considered, the normative (and self-interested) reason that I have to take a nap is outweighed by the weightier normative (and moral) reason that I have to keep my promise. But now consider a different version of the case. Suppose that right before our planned meeting I accidentally cracked a tooth. And let's suppose that the pain is excruciating. What's more, I'll have to pay thousands of dollars extra to get it fixed at an emergency dental clinic this weekend if I don't get it fixed before my regular in-network dentist closes this afternoon. But if I'm to get it taken care of right away, I'll have to miss my appointment with the student (and there's no way for me to let them know beforehand). In this variant of the case, it seems that the normative (and self-interested) reasons that I have to do what will save me both hours of agony and the loss of thousands of dollars outweighs the normative (and moral) reasons that I have to keep my promise. Thus, contrary to what the normative pluralist claims, it seems quite sensible to think that there is a fact about what I just plain ought to do in these cases in which various qualified oughts conflict.[16]

So there seems to be two kinds of normativity. On one hand, there's qualified normativity, which concerns what we ought to do in various qualified senses: for example, what we legally, morally, or self-interestedly ought to do. On the other hand, there's unqualified normativity, which concerns what we just plain ought to do – or, in other words, what we ought to do, all things (and, thus, all reasons) considered. This kind of normativity is unqualified such that those who fail to do as they ought to do in this sense are guilty of having responded inappropriately to their reasons.

Given this distinction between qualified and unqualified normativity, we can distinguish between qualified and unqualified (normative) reasons. First, there are qualified (normative) reasons, which are considerations that are relevant to what we qualifiedly ought to do. And different kinds of qualified reasons count for or against different kinds of qualified oughts. For instance, a *moral* reason for or against a subject's φ-ing in circumstances C is any fact that counts for or against φ's being how they morally ought to respond in C. A *self-interested*

---

[16] But see Mathias Sagdahl (2014) for a response.

reason for or against their φ-ing in C is any fact that counts for or against φ's being how they self-interestedly ought to respond in C. And an *aesthetic* reason for or against their φ-ing in C is any fact that counts for or against φ's being how they aesthetically ought to respond in C. Second, there are unqualified (normative) reasons, which are considerations that combine and compete to determine what we just plain ought to do – that is, what we ought to do, all things considered. More generally, a D reason for φ-ing ("D" standing for some domain such as "moral," "legal," or "unqualified") makes φ-ing more D-ly choiceworthy and a D reason against φ-ing makes φ-ing less D-ly choiceworthy. Of course, a reason can be both a qualified and an unqualified reason. For instance, the fact that I would be better off taking care of my cavity right away seems not only to be a self-interested reason for me to do so but also an unqualified reason for me to do so. That is, this consideration seems relevant in determining both what I self-interestedly ought to do and what I just plain ought to do. And, whenever I use the word "reason," I'm talking about unqualified reasons – unless, of course, I explicitly use some qualifier such as "moral" or "legal."

2.3 Normative Reasons versus Normatively Relevant Facts

We've seen that a normative reason for (or against) a subject's φ-ing counts for (or against) φ's being what they ought to do. But normative reasons are not the only normatively relevant facts, where a *normatively relevant fact* with respect to a subject's φ-ing is just any fact that's relevant to whether they ought to φ. Likewise, moral reasons are not the only morally relevant facts, where a *morally relevant fact* with respect to a subject's φ-ing is just any fact that's relevant to whether they morally ought to φ. In general, for any qualified or unqualified normative domain D, a *D reason* for (or against) a subject's φ-ing counts for (or against) φ's being what they D-ly ought to do, whereas a *D-ly relevant fact* with respect to a subject's φ-ing is any fact that's relevant to whether they D-ly ought to φ. Now, clearly, any D reason for (or against) a subject's φ-ing will be a D-ly relevant fact with respect to their φ-ing, but, as I've just indicated, not every D-ly relevant fact with respect to a subject's φ-ing will be a D reason for (or against) their φ-ing—see Figure 1.

To illustrate, suppose both that each agent morally ought to produce the greatest balance of pleasure over pain for others that they can produce without violating anyone's rights and that each agent has a right not to be slapped by others but no right not to be slapped by themself. On this moral view, the fact that the face that I'm slapping is my own is a morally relevant fact with respect to my slapping this face, but it's not a moral reason for or against my slapping it.

It's a morally relevant fact given that it morally justifies my slapping this face. But the fact that the face that I'm slapping is my own is not a moral reason for or against my slapping it. After all, it counts neither for nor against this being what I morally ought to do. For, on the given moral view, the only thing that counts for an act's being one that I morally ought to perform is that it will either increase someone else's pleasure or decrease someone else's pain. And the only thing that counts against an act's being something that I morally ought to perform is that it will increase someone else's pain, decrease someone else's pleasure, or violate someone's rights. Of course, I'm not suggesting that this is a plausible moral view. The point is only to illustrate how, on certain moral views, not every morally relevant fact will constitute a moral reason.

Here's another example. The fact that I *can* touch my nose is neither a normative reason for nor against my doing so. For the mere fact that this is something I can do neither favors nor disfavors my doing so. Nevertheless, this fact is relevant to whether I ought to touch my nose, because "ought" implies "can" such that one ought to φ only if one can φ – or, at least, let's assume this for the sake of argument. Thus, touching my nose can be something that I ought to do only if it's something that I can do. So if I were paralyzed and consequently unable to touch my nose, touching my nose wouldn't be something that I ought to do no matter how great it would be for me to do so. The fact that I'm able to touch my nose is therefore a normatively relevant fact with respect to my touching my nose, but it's not a normative reason for or against my touching my nose – thus, it's a *normatively relevant non-reason* with respect to my touching my nose.

The distinction between a *D reason* for or against a subject's φ-ing and a *D-ly relevant non-reason* with respect to their φ-ing applies across various normative domains, including the epistemic domain. Thus, someone might hold that whether one should believe that *p* depends not only on how much evidence one has for *p*'s being true but also how much is at stake for one with regard to whether *p* is true.[17] To illustrate, consider the following example.

> *The Layover*: Hector is at the Houston airport contemplating taking a certain flight to New York. He wants to know whether the flight has a layover in Atlanta. Peeking over another passenger's shoulder (a passenger named Louise), he sees that her itinerary clearly states that the flight has a layover in Atlanta. But whereas Louise doesn't really care where the layover is, Hector does. For Hector has a very important business contact he has to

---

[17] I realize that most epistemologists think that the stakes are relevant only with respect to whether one counts as knowing a proposition and not with respect to whether one ought to believe that proposition, but the point of this example is only to illustrate the distinction between normative reasons and normatively relevant facts.

meet at the Atlanta airport. Hector wonders: "How reliable is this itinerary? It could contain a misprint. Or the airline could have changed the schedule since it was printed." Thus, Hector decides to check with the gate agent to see whether the flight does indeed stop in Atlanta.[18]

It seems that, initially, Hector and Louise have the exact same evidence with regard to whether the flight stops in Atlanta: the fact that the itinerary clearly states that the flight has a layover in Atlanta. But someone might think that whereas Louise ought on this basis to believe that it stops in Atlanta, Hector shouldn't. Given the high stakes for him and the possibility of misprints and last-minute schedule changes, he shouldn't believe that it's going to Atlanta without first confirming this with the gate agent. Louise, by contrast, should believe that it's going to stop in Atlanta despite the slight possibility of misprints and last-minute schedule changes given that the stakes are quite low for her. So, in *The Layover*, it may be that, on certain epistemic theories, how high the stakes are for one in whether the flight stops in Atlanta is doxastically relevant with respect to whether one ought to believe that it does, and yet whether the stakes are high or low counts neither for nor against believing that it does. For the fact that the stakes are high or low doesn't count as evidence for or against the flight's stopping in Atlanta. Thus, it's neither a reason for nor a reason against believing that it will stop in Atlanta. Thus, it's a doxastically relevant fact with respect to whether one ought to believe that it stops in Atlanta, but it's not a doxastic reason to believe that it does. Thus it's a normatively relevant non-reason with respect to believing that it stops in Atlanta.

Normatively relevant non-reasons divide into six types. Two of these types are *enablers* and *nullifiers*. An enabler is a fact that enables some other fact that wouldn't otherwise count as a reason to count as a reason.[19] To illustrate, the fact that it would be good if a doctor were to give a boy a shot of penicillin counts as a reason for them to do so only if they can give him such a shot. After all, it seems that "S has a reason to φ" implies that "S can φ" (see Streumer 2007). Thus the fact that they can give the boy such a shot counts as an enabler. Although the fact that they can give him a shot of penicillin is not itself a reason to do so, it's what enables the fact that it would be good if they were to give him such a shot to constitute a reason for them to do so.

---

[18] This is based off a similar example from Stew Cohen (1999, p. 58).

[19] As with the other types to follow, enablers can be reasons as well as non-reasons. That is, the fact that enables some other fact that wouldn't otherwise count as a reason to count as a reason could itself be a reason. For the sake of brevity, I illustrate each type in terms of non-reasons only. But keep in mind that it's not just non-reasons that can divide into enablers, nullifiers, and such; reasons can too.

There are also nullifiers. For instance, some think that the fact that I've promised not to let my self-interested concerns influence my decision about which candidate to recommend to the department prevents the fact that I would personally benefit from recommending a given candidate from counting in favor of my recommending them to the department. They take it to be a nullifier in that it prevents the fact that I would personally benefit from recommending them to the department (a fact that would otherwise count in favor of my doing so) from counting in favor of my doing so.[20]

Two other types of normatively relevant non-reasons are *intensifiers* and *attenuators*. To illustrate, suppose that I come across, on an infrequently traveled road, a man who is struggling to change his vehicle's flat tire. The fact that I'm the only one who can help him seems to intensify the reason I have to stop and help him, but the fact that it's entirely his fault that he's in this predicament (because, say, he didn't get new tires even though I'd told him last month that he needed them) seems to attenuate my reason to stop and help him (Dancy 2006b, p. 49).

Last, there are *justifiers* and *counter-justifiers*: facts that make it easier or harder to justify responding in a certain way, respectively. For instance, the fact that it's *my* face that I'm slapping may morally justify my slapping this face, but it doesn't morally count in favor of my doing so. Thus it's a moral justifier, but not a moral reason. That is, it's a fact that justifies my slapping this face, making it permissible for me do so, but without in any way making it more morally choiceworthy for me to do so.

And there are counter-justifiers: facts that make it harder to justify responding in certain ways. To illustrate, recall *The Layover*. As noted earlier, one might want to say that although Hector and Louise have the exact same doxastic reasons for believing that the flight will stop in Atlanta, these reasons are sufficient for Louise to believe that it will do so but insufficient for Hector to believe that it will do so given that the stakes are much higher for Hector than for Louise. And if this is right, then the high stakes would be a counter-justifier. That is, the fact that the stakes are quite high for Hector would be a counter-justifier for Hector's believing that the flight will stop in Atlanta.

In this section, I've argued that there is an important distinction between a fact that counts D-ly in favor of one's φ-ing and a fact that is relevant to whether one D-ly ought to φ. And although every D-reason for or against one's φ-ing is relevant to whether one D-ly ought to φ, not every fact that is relevant

---

[20] And there are likely important differences between a fact's nullifying the reason-giving force that some other fact would otherwise have and a fact's outweighing the reason-giving force that some other fact retains. For instance, it seems that if the would-be force of a fact is nullified, then you wouldn't even need any reasons to countervail its nonexisting force.

to whether one D-ly ought to φ is a D reason for or against one's φ-ing. What's more, I explained how there are various different sorts of normatively relevant facts: enablers, nullifiers, intensifiers, attenuators, justifiers, and counter-justifiers.

2.4 Moral Reasons versus Nonmoral Reasons

Despite the importance of the distinction that I've just explicated in the previous section, philosophers have often conflated morally relevant facts with moral reasons. For instance, Walter Sinnott-Armstrong (1992, p. 403) claims: "Since a reason for action is a fact that can affect the rationality of an act, a moral reason is a fact that can affect the morality of an act, either by making an otherwise morally neutral act morally good or by making an otherwise immoral act moral." But the fact that it's my face that I'm slapping can make an otherwise immoral act (e.g., the act of my slapping someone's face) moral, but it's not a moral reason for or against my doing so. Thus it affects the moral status of an act, but it isn't something that counts for or against that act, morally speaking.

Shelly Kagan also conflates a morally relevant fact with a moral reason. He holds that if "we are concerned with what is required by morality, the relevant reasons – whether decisive or not – must be moral ones" (1989, p. 66). Now, if we're concerned with what is required by morality, then the relevant reasons must be *morally relevant reasons*, but they needn't be *moral reasons* – that is, they needn't be considerations that count for or against some response, *morally speaking*. For although all moral reasons must be morally relevant reasons, not all morally relevant reasons are moral reasons. To illustrate, consider the following case.

> *The Trivial Promise*: I've promised to meet with a student to discuss their exam grade from the past semester. But subsequent to my making this promise, I learn of a golden opportunity to take a free trip around the world on a luxury sailing yacht – something both that I've always dreamed of doing and that would normally cost many hundreds of thousands of dollars. Unfortunately, if I'm to take advantage of this opportunity, I must immediately drive down to the city to sign up before the offer expires. But this will mean missing my appointment with the student, and I have no way of contacting them beforehand. In the end, I decide to drive down to the city and sign up for the free trip. But I apologize profusely to the student when I get back, making sure to pay them sufficient restitution to more than compensate for any frustration or inconvenience that I've caused them. What's more, I go out of my way to reschedule our meeting at their earliest convenience.

In this case, it seems that the reason that I had to drive down to the city (that doing so will get me a free trip around the world on a luxury sailing yacht) was a nonmoral reason, for it doesn't seem to make my driving down to the city morally choiceworthy (or morally unchoiceworthy) in any respect.[21] Yet this nonmoral reason was morally relevant because it did make an otherwise morally impermissible act (that of missing my appointment) morally permissible. Of course I was required to make it up to the student, but it wasn't wrong for me to miss our appointment given that this was the only way for me to fulfill my lifelong dream of sailing around the world. Thus the self-interested reason that I had to drive down to the city to sign up for the free trip seems to be a *morally relevant nonmoral reason* – and see Figure 2 for how this notion relates to the other notions that we've been talking about.

Now, Joshua Gert thinks that "the phrase 'morally relevant non-moral reason' should raise some eyebrows" (2014, p. 211). He wonders: "Why should we not grant that if a consideration is capable of providing moral justification, then this shows that it does count, morally, in favour of an option?" (p. 211). The answer is that we should not grant this because morally *justifying* is not at all the same thing as morally *favoring*. The fact that it's my face that I'm slapping may morally justify what I'm doing (viz., slapping this face), but it doesn't morally favor my doing so. That is, the fact that it's my face that I'm slapping doesn't speak in favor of my slapping this face, morally speaking. Indeed, it does nothing to make my slapping this face morally choiceworthy. So, however we draw the distinction between moral reasons and nonmoral reasons, we must be careful not to conflate moral reasons with morally relevant reasons, as Gert, Kagan, and Sinnott-Armstrong have done.

So morally relevant reasons are (moral or nonmoral) reasons that are relevant to the moral status of a response. These (moral or nonmoral) reasons can be morally relevant either because they morally favor/disfavor that response or because they serve merely as a moral enabler, a moral defeater, a moral intensifier, a moral attenuator, a moral justifier, or a moral counter-justifier.[22] Those that are morally relevant because they morally favor or disfavor are moral reasons, and those that are morally relevant because they merely serve as a

---

[21] Assume that if I don't take advantage of this offer, this will only free up a spot for someone who is even more deserving of this opportunity. So, if anything, it seems that I have a moral reason to free up this spot for this more deserving someone. Admittedly, the reason that I have to drive down to the city (that doing so will get me a free trip around the world on a luxury sailing yacht) would count as a moral reason on a theory such as classical utilitarianism, but I'm talking about how things *seem*, not how things *are alleged to be on some contentious moral theory*.

[22] Not only can non-reasons be moral justifiers, but so too can nonmoral reasons. The fact that the face that I'm slapping is my own is a non-reason for me to slap this face that morally justifies my doing so. By contrast, the fact that my pleasure would be increased by my driving down to the city and signing up for the free trip in *The Trivial Promise* is a reason (a nonmoral reason, it seems) for me to do so that morally justifies my doing this instead of keeping my promise.

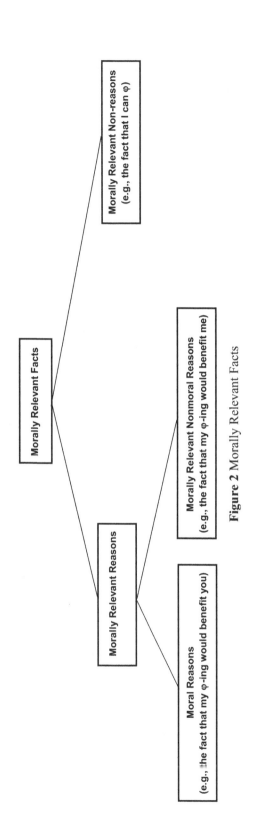

Figure 2 Morally Relevant Facts

moral enabler or the like are morally relevant nonmoral reasons. More precisely, the two can be defined as follows.

Moral Reasons: For any subject S with the option of φ-ing in circumstances C, a moral reason *for* S to φ in C is any fact that will, absent its morally favoring force being defeated, make it the case that they morally ought to φ in C. Likewise, a moral reason *against* S's φ-ing in C is any fact that will, absent its morally disfavoring force being defeated, make it the case that they morally ought not to φ in C.[23] And a nonmoral reason is any reason that's not a moral reason.[24]

Morally Relevant Nonmoral Reasons: For any subject S with the option of φ-ing in circumstances C, a morally relevant nonmoral reason for or against S's φ-ing in C is any nonmoral reason that's relevant to whether or not they morally ought to φ in C given that it serves as a moral enabler, a moral defeater, a moral intensifier, a moral attenuator, a moral justifier, or a moral counter-justifier.

Of course, just because there's a distinction between two kinds of things doesn't mean that it's a useful or important one. There's a distinction between live rabbits with hearts and live rabbits without hearts, but it's not a very useful distinction given that all actual live rabbits have hearts. Perhaps the distinction between moral reasons and nonmoral reasons is like this. Perhaps all reasons are moral reasons. This view is sometimes called *moralism*.[25] Another possibility is that all reasons are nonmoral reasons. And we can call this view *anti-moralism*. I think that neither view is plausible. Contrary to moralism, the fact that I get more pleasure from drinking Coke than I do from drinking Pepsi seems to be a nonmoral reason for me to drink Coke instead of Pepsi. It seems to be a nonmoral reason, for the mere fact that I get more pleasure from drinking Coke doesn't seem to make my choosing Coke over Pepsi in any way morally

---

[23] Stephen Darwall has suggested that "moral reasons ... are *pro tanto* moral obligation-making considerations. They are facts that tend to make an act morally obligatory" (2017, p. 1). But some moral reasons (e.g., the reason that I have to smile at the student whom I pass in the hall given that this will slightly cheer them) seem to have the power to make this an act that I morally ought to perform without having the power to make this one that I'm morally obligated to perform. So I think that, contrary to Darwall, we should think that moral reasons are *pro tanto* moral *ought-making* considerations, not *pro tanto* moral *obligation-making* considerations.

[24] What distinguishes moral reasons from nonmoral reasons is neither that the two have distinctive grounds (e.g., the former is and the latter isn't grounded in our social practices) nor that the two have distinctive contents (e.g., the former is and the latter isn't other-regarding). Rather, what distinguishes the two is their distinctive functional roles. Moral reasons, unlike nonmoral reasons, function to generate moral oughts when their favoring forces remain undefeated. See Forcehimes and Semrau 2018 for difficulties with those approaches that instead appeal either to their putative distinctive grounds or to their putative distinctive contents.

[25] See, for instance, Haldane 2011, who's a proponent.

choiceworthy. After all, it doesn't seem that choosing Coke over Pepsi is what I *morally* ought to do even if it is what I *self-interestedly* ought to do.[26]

And, contrary to anti-moralism, the fact (if it is a fact) that the Pepsi corporation treats its workers better than the Coca-Cola corporation treats its workers seems to be a moral reason to purchase stock in Pepsi instead of Coke. So it seems that there are reasons of both the moral and nonmoral varieties. What's more, the distinction between moral and nonmoral reasons would seem to be an important one, for, as I'll argue later in this Element, both types of reasons are relevant in determining how we (just plain) ought to live. Indeed, these two types of reasons can support conflicting answers to the question of how we ought to live. For instance, it could be that I have a nonmoral reason to choose Coke over Pepsi but a moral reason to choose Pepsi over Coke.[27]

3 Are Moral Reasons Unqualified (Normative) Reasons?

We've seen that moral reasons are, by definition, relevant to what we morally ought to do. But are moral reasons also relevant to what we just plain ought to do? That is, are they merely qualified (normative) reasons, or are they also unqualified (normative) reasons? This is an important question because moral reasons are relevant to answering the all-important question of how we (just plain) ought to live only if they are unqualified reasons.

On the face of it, moral reasons seem to be unqualified reasons, for they seem to combine and compete with other unqualified reasons to determine what we just plain ought to do. For instance, the fact that my pulling a drowning child out of the pool would save their life seems to count in favor of this being not only what I morally ought to do, but also what I just plain ought to do. Thus, if I don't have any strong reason not to pull them out of the pool, then this will be what I ought to do, all things considered. Self-interested reasons are also, on the face of it, unqualified reasons. If I have a self-interested reason to go to the dentist, then,

---

[26] The claim is not that there can never be a moral reason to promote one's self-interest, neither is the claim that there are never any self-regarding moral reasons. The claim is only that the mere fact that φ-ing would promote one's self-interest is not itself a moral reason for one to φ, for the fact that φ-ing would, say, increase one's hedonic utility, increasing the net sum of pleasure over pain that one experiences, doesn't itself count as a moral reason for one to φ even though it does entail that φ-ing would promote one's self-interest. Of course, promoting one's own self-interest can derivatively count as a moral reason, as where decreasing one's self-interest would interfere with one's mental health to an extent that would impede one's ability to act morally in the future, but, strictly speaking, it's the fact that φ-ing would enhance one's ability to act morally in the future and not the fact that φ-ing would promote one's self-interest that counts a moral reason for one to φ. I have more to say on this topic in Section 3.3.

[27] Of course, some have historically tried to argue that these two never conflict on the grounds that being moral is always in one's self-interest (see, e.g., Plato's *Republic*). Unfortunately, these arguments are unconvincing.

absent the favoring force of this reason being defeated, this will be not only what I self-interestedly ought to do but also what I ought to do, all things considered.

In this respect, moral reasons and self-interested reasons seem to differ from etiquettal reasons. For etiquettal reasons seem to be merely qualified reasons. Thus, although the fact that my eating with my elbows on the table is bad table manners seems relevant to whether I etiquettally ought to do so, it doesn't seem relevant to whether I just plain ought to do so. Indeed, it seems that dining etiquette is relevant to what I have unqualified reason to do only insofar as I have some unqualified reason to abide by dining etiquette – as I would have if, say, someone at my table would be offended by my flouting such rules. But even then, the unqualified reason that I would have to refrain from eating with my elbows on the table would not be the etiquettal reason that I have to abide by dining etiquette, but the moral reason that I have to refrain from needlessly offending someone. Now, as it happens, no one at my table cares about good table manners, and so no one would be offended by my eating with my elbows on the table. So, although I make a mistake from the point of view of etiquette when I eat with my elbows on the table, I don't fail to respond appropriately to my (unqualified) reasons in doing so. After all, I have no (unqualified) reason to refrain from eating with my elbows on the table. Thus etiquettal reasons count for or against an act's being what I etiquettally ought to do, but not for or against an act's being what I just plain ought to do.

3.1 Subjectivism

Although moral reasons, unlike etiquettal reasons, certainly seem to be unqualified reasons, some philosophers have argued that things are not as they seem. For instance, Philippa Foot has argued that moral reasons are not themselves unqualified reasons. She's argued that just as etiquettal reasons provide us with unqualified reasons only insofar as we have some unqualified reason to follow the rules of etiquette, moral reasons provide us with unqualified reasons only insofar as we have some unqualified reason to follow the rules of morality. And she has claimed, in general, that only those who care about following a particular set of rules have any unqualified reason to do so. Thus she believes that those who reject the rules of morality have no (unqualified) reason to abide by them. She has argued as follows:

> The fact is that the man who rejects morality because he sees no reason to obey its rules can be convicted of villainy but not of inconsistency. Nor will his action necessarily be irrational. Irrational actions are those in which a man in some way defeats his own purposes, doing what is calculated to be disadvantageous or to frustrate his ends. Immorality does not necessarily involve any such thing. (Foot 1972, p. 310)

The problem, though, is that Foot hasn't shown that we don't have any unqualified reason to act as we're morally required to act. If anything, she's shown only that it can be rationally coherent – involving no inconsistency in one's attitudes – to fail to act as morality demands (Worsnip Forthcoming). But to show that there need be no inconsistency in one's attitudes when one fails to act as one is morally required to act is not to show that the moral reasons grounding this moral requirement are not unqualified reasons. For even if the cruel person needn't be guilty of any inconsistency, it may be that they are, nonetheless, failing to respond appropriately to the unqualified reasons that they have not to be cruel.

So it seems that Foot must have been assuming a kind of subjectivism about unqualified reasons. That is, she must have been assuming that one has an unqualified reason to refrain from being cruel only if one happens to have a concern for not being cruel. More carefully, "subjectivism about [unqualified] reasons for action is the thesis that only an agent's contingent concerns ultimately ground her" unqualified reasons for action (Sobel 2016, p. 219). Thus "subjectivists agree that if one has a[n unqualified] reason to [φ], that reason can only be grounded by the fact that [φ]-ing would serve some contingent concern or other" (Sobel 2016, p. 219).

To have a (positive) concern for something is to have a pro-attitude toward it. And a pro-attitude is just any attitude that favors its object – attitudes such as liking, valuing, admiring, desiring, approving, and preferring. These attitudes favor their objects in that they dispose their subjects to find them attractive or appealing and to consequently choose, pursue, or promote them if able to.[28] For instance, my liking Coke more than Pepsi disposes me to find the prospect of drinking Coke more appealing than that of drinking Pepsi and to consequently choose Coke over Pepsi when I have the choice between the two. So something serves one's contingent concerns only insofar as it serves to effect one's getting, achieving, or promoting the objects of one's contingent pro-attitudes.

By "contingent," subjectivists don't mean "metaphysically contingent." The idea isn't merely that it's metaphysically possible for the subject to lack the given concern or pro-attitude. For the relevant sort of contingency is rational contingency. Thus a contingent concern or pro-attitude is just one that the subject isn't rationally required to have.[29] And what makes a concern or pro-attitude contingent in this sense is that there are no unqualified reasons requiring

---

[28] A favoring attitude is more than just a disposition to act so as to promote its object. It must additionally dispose its subject to find its object attractive or appealing.

[29] I use the following phrases interchangeably: "is required to φ," "is rationally required to φ," "is normatively required to φ," "is unqualifiedly required to φ," "is required by reasons to φ," "has decisive (unqualified) reason to φ," and "is required, all things considered, to φ."

the subject to have it. For instance, there's no unqualified reason for me to like Coke more than Pepsi. I just do; it's just a contingent fact about myself that I happen to enjoy the taste of Coke more than that of Pepsi. But other people enjoy the taste of Pepsi more than that of Coke. And it's not that some of us are being unresponsive to reasons in liking the one more than the other. It's just that different people often happen to have different rationally acceptable likes. Now, the fact that likings are rationally contingent is uncontroversial. But whether all pro-attitudes, including desires, are also rationally contingent is controversial. Those known as Humeans (given that they follow David Hume on this issue) think that no pro-attitude is rationally assessable. They claim that there are never any unqualified reasons for having or lacking a particular pro-attitude, such as a particular desire or preference. Indeed, Hume famously said: "'Tis not contrary to reason to prefer the destruction of the whole world to the scratching of my finger" (1739, bk. 2, pt. 3). Others, known as anti-Humeans, think that the fact that you would be much better off if your finger was scratched than if the whole world (with you in it) were destroyed is an unqualified reason for you to prefer the scratching of your finger. But we needn't resolve the issue here because we can just formulate subjectivism in terms of rationally contingent pro-attitudes and leave open whether these include only a subset of pro-attitudes (perhaps only likings) or all pro-attitudes (including both likings and desires). Thus we can formulate the relevant view as follows.

> **Subjectivism:** For any subject S and any act available to them φ, S has a reason (that is, an unqualified reason) to φ if and only if their φ-ing would serve to satisfy some rationally contingent pro-attitude of theirs. And if S has a reason (that is, an unqualified reason) to φ, it's ultimately due to the fact that their φ-ing would serve to satisfy some rationally contingent pro-attitude of theirs.[30]

Subjectivism, as even subjectivists themselves admit, has various problematic features (Sobel 2016, p. 11). Perhaps the most serious of these is that it cannot accommodate our intuition that moral reasons are unqualified reasons (Sobel 2016, p. 17).[31] For instance, it seems that we all necessarily have a moral and an unqualified reason to refrain from torturing the innocent and that this is ultimately because doing so would cause tremendous physical and

---

[30] A lot of what I say in what follows concerning subjectivism is indebted to Derek Parfit's work on this topic. See, for instance, his 1997 and his 2011.

[31] According to the subjectivist, the fact that torturing the innocent causes underserved suffering (which is itself a moral reason against torturing the innocent) is not itself an unqualified reason against torturing the innocent. For the subjectivist holds that what would constitute an unqualified reason against torturing the innocent is only that doing so would serve to dissatisfy some rationally contingent pro-attitude of the agent – such as their just happening to dislike seeing people suffer.

psychological suffering to those who don't deserve to so suffer. Yet the subject-ivist can't guarantee that we all have such a reason, neithers can they hold that, for those who do have such a reason, it's ultimately because torturing the innocent would cause tremendous physical and psychological suffering to those who don't deserve to suffer. Instead, the subjectivist must hold that only those who happen to have a rationally contingent pro-attitude that would be served by refraining from torturing the innocent have an unqualified reason to refrain from doing so. And the subjectivist must hold that their reason to so refrain ultimately has nothing to do with how torture affects its victims, but has only to do with how it will affect the torturer by either serving or failing to serve their rationally contingent pro-attitudes. What's worse, the subjectivist must hold that if a subject has some rationally contingent pro-attitude that would be satisfied by torturing the innocent (if, for instance, they like the experience of torturing) and no rationally contingent pro-attitude that would be dissatisfied by torturing the innocent, then they just plain ought to torture the innocent. And even today's leading proponents of subjectivism admit that this is a problem. For they admit that intuitively it seems that "we have significant reasons to not, for example, abuse the vulnerable regardless of our concerns." And they admit that "subjectivism ... cannot guarantee that all agents have such reasons" (Sobel 2016, p. 17).

Of course just because subjectivism has certain problematic features doesn't mean that we should reject it. For it may have fewer or less serious problematic features than any alternative position does. As Sobel points out: "Those who have done philosophy for a while are used to the unsettling reality that the attempt to systematize our thinking in an area almost always forces us to abandon or explain away some features that felt intuitive" (2016, p. 21). So ultimately subjectivists want to argue that although subjectivism forces us to abandon the intuition that we all necessarily have an unqualified reason to refrain from torturing the innocent, subjectivism does a better job of system-atizing all of our intuitions than any alternative position does. That is, they want to argue that the merits of subjectivism outweigh its demerits, including the demerit of its not being able to account for our intuition that at least some moral reasons (e.g., the moral reason that we have to refrain from torturing the innocent) are unqualified reasons.[32]

---

[32] As some see it, one of the chief advantages of subjectivism is that it allows us to hold that the normative is ultimately grounded in (and thus reduced to) the nonnormative. I don't find such reductive accounts of the normative plausible, but I admit that the issue is far from settled. What's more, a lot of interesting work has been done on this issue that I can't even begin to address here. So, for a contrary point of view, the reader should see, for instance, Schroeder (2007).

3.2 Matters of Mere Taste

What, then, are the merits of subjectivism? One thing that supposedly counts in subjectivism's favor is its putative ability to provide the simplest and most straightforward account of our reasons concerning matters of mere taste. Thus subjectivists contend that their view does the best job of accounting for the reason that I, for instance, have to drink Coke rather than Pepsi given that I like the taste of Coke more than I like the taste of Pepsi. What accounts for this? Their answer is simple and straightforward: what we have reason to do ultimately depends on what our rationally contingent pro-attitudes (such as our likings) are.

Of course being able to account for our reasons concerning matters of mere taste constitutes an advantage for the subjectivist only if there is no alternative theory that can provide an account that is at least as plausible. So let's consider the following alternative.

> **Desire Objectivism:** For any subject S and any act available to them φ, S has a reason (that is, an unqualified reason) to φ if and only if their φ-ing would serve to satisfy some desire that they are rationally required to have (and, thus, one that's not rationally contingent). And if S has a reason (that is, an unqualified reason) to φ, it's ultimately due to the fact that their φ-ing would serve to satisfy some desire that they are rationally required to have.[33]

The desire objectivist can account for our reasons concerning matters of mere taste if they assume both that we're rationally required (that is, required by our unqualified reasons) to desire the state of affairs in which we experience a sensation that we like having and that we're required to prefer the state of affairs in which we experience a sensation that we like having more to one in which we experience a sensation that we like having less. Thus, the explanation for why I have more reason to drink Coke than to drink Pepsi is ultimately that this will satisfy a preference that I'm required to have: the preference for the state of affairs in which I experience a sensation that I like having more (that of drinking Coke) to one in which I experience a sensation that I like having less (that of drinking Pepsi). So the subjectivist and the objectivist agree both that I have a reason to drink Coke rather than Pepsi and that this is grounded in my rationally contingent preference for the taste of Coke over the taste of Pepsi, but they disagree on what *ultimately* grounds this reason. Whereas the subjectivist holds that it's that the *nonnormative* fact that I happen to have a rationally contingent preference for the taste of Coke over the taste of Pepsi, the objectivist holds that it is instead the *normative* fact that I'm required to prefer the state of

---

[33] For a further defense of this view, see my 2011 (chap. 3).

affairs in which I experience a sensation that I contingently like more to the state of affairs in which I experience a sensation that I contingently like less.

But which view provides the better ultimate explanation? I believe that it's desire objectivism. The problem with subjectivism's explanation is that it implausibly implies that attitudes that we have no reason to have could be the ultimate source of our practical reasons. To see why this is implausible, imagine that I have a brain disorder with the following three effects: (1) I can no longer rid myself of a desire to eat by eating and so have a constant desire to eat unless medicated, (2) the only way for me to rid myself of a desire to eat is by taking an 86 pill (note that "to eighty-six" is North American slang that can mean "to get rid of"), a pill that gets rid of any desire to eat and lasts eight hours, and (3) I can receive no pleasure from eating.[34] Now let's suppose that it's been more than eight hours since I last took an 86 pill and consequently I desire to eat even though I've just eaten a large and nutritious meal. And let's suppose that this is a noninstrumental desire. Thus I desire to eat, not because I believe that this will satiate my desire to eat or give me pleasure (I know that it won't), but simply because I find the prospect of my eating for the sake of eating inherently attractive. Last, let's suppose that I lack any noninstrumental desire to take an 86 pill – that is, I want to take an 86 pill only because I know that it will get rid of my desire to eat. Now, in this case, it seems that I have no reason to eat. Eating won't give me pleasure. And it won't provide me with any health benefits, as I've already eaten a large and nutritious meal. Yet eating would satisfy my rationally contingent desire to eat for the sake of eating. So subjectivism implies I have a reason to eat. But this is implausible, for it seems that I might as well just get rid of my desire to eat by taking an 86 pill rather than fulfilling it by eating. Since there's no reason for me to have this desire, it seems that fulfilling it is no better than getting rid of it.

Thus it seems that the fact that my φ-ing would satisfy some rationally contingent desire of mine is not itself a reason for me to φ. Rather, if I have a reason to satisfy my rationally contingent desire by φ-ing, it's only a derivative reason. That is, I would have a reason to do so only in virtue of the fact that in doing so I would, say, obtain pleasure or avoid pain.

In sum, desire objectivism seems to offer the more plausible account of our reasons concerning matters of mere taste. For the desire objectivist holds that

---

[34] I'm open to pleasures being either (a) sensations that have a certain phenomenological flavor or dimension or (b) sensations that their subjects like in virtue of the way that they feel. In either case, I claim that subjects are rationally required to desire such sensations and that they have reason to pursue such sensations ultimately because doing so would serve to satisfy such a rationally required desire. That such subjects are rationally required to desire such sensations and have a reason to satisfy such desires is, I believe, just a brute normative fact.

what ultimately grounds my reason to choose Coke over Pepsi is the *normative* fact that I ought to prefer the state of affairs in which I have an experience that I like more to the one in which I have an experience that I like less, whereas the subjectivist holds that what ultimately grounds my reason to choose Coke over Pepsi is the *nonnormative* fact that I happen to like the taste of Coke more than that of Pepsi.

3.3 The Non-alienation Constraint

Another thing that subjectivists believe counts in favor of their view is that it supposedly best accounts for the following constraint on (practical) reasons.

> **The Non-alienation Constraint:** For any fact F, any subject S, and any act available to them φ, F is a reason (that is, an unqualified reason) for S to φ only if S wouldn't find this intolerably alienating in the appropriate circumstances.

David Sobel, for instance, makes the point as follows: "subjectivism has a very good story of in what sense my reasons are built to suit me. I can hardly be alienated from my entire conative set" (2016, p. 36). But it seems to me that we can indeed be alienated from our entire set of *rationally contingent* pro-attitudes and that what we can't be alienated from is only our *rationally required* pro-attitudes. Thus I think that, if anything, the non-alienation constraint actually favors desire objectivism when we properly interpret the phrase "in the appropriate circumstances."

Consider that upon reflection I feel alienated from many if not all of my rationally contingent pro-attitudes. For I often find that these rationally contingent pro-attitudes conflict with the desires that I have reason to have. For instance, I have a sweet tooth even though my blood sugar levels are higher than they should be. I gather this is because when my hominid ancestors evolved, calories were often in short supply and sweet things tended to be loaded with needed calories. But now I find myself in a world with easy access to calories, including heavily refined sweets with no nutritional value, and so I find myself with a desire for something that's bad for me – a desire that I'm required to wish that I lacked. Consider also that I enjoy watching mixed martial arts. Yet upon reflection I can't see any reason why I should want to watch two people needlessly beat each other up. But again I assume that there is some evolutionary explanation for why I'm entertained by such displays of violence. But upon reflection I find only reasons to disvalue such violence. Last, take the case of my liking the taste of Coke more than I do the taste of Pepsi. Although this liking doesn't conflict with my values, it also doesn't reflect who I am in any deep or important sense. It just seems to be an arbitrary fact about my physiology – one that has nothing to do with anything that I have reason to care about. Thus this liking seems alien to me *qua* rational subject, which is how I conceive of myself.

In all such cases, then, I find myself having rationally contingent pro-attitudes that I have absolutely no reason to have. And again, when I reflect on this, I find this alienating given that these pro-attitudes always fail to reflect (and sometimes even conflict with) my values – that which I see myself as having reason to desire.[35] What's more, it seems possible for *all* my rationally contingent pro-attitudes to be alienating in this way. So it seems to me entirely possible, contrary to Sobel's claim, for someone to be alienated from their entire set of rationally contingent pro-attitudes.

Given this, it seems to me that the desire objectivist is again in a better position to account for the constraint in question. For it seems to me that the appropriate circumstances are the ones in which I reflect on whether my rationally contingent pro-attitudes reflect the values and desires that I would have if I were relevantly informed and substantively rational.[36] And, in those circumstances, I find many (if not all) of the rationally contingent pro-attitudes that I just happen to have to be alienating. But I don't find any of the pro-attitudes that I ought to have (such as the desire that I have to protect my child) to be alienating. So it's the desire objectivist, not the subjectivist, that can best account for the non-alienation constraint when properly understood. For it's the desire objectivist rather than the subjectivist that holds that what ultimately grounds my reasons is something that I cannot feel alienated from given that I, *qua* rational agent, can't feel alienated from the preferences that I'm required to have in the way that I do feel alienated from the rationally contingent preferences that I just happen to have. What's more, the desire objectivist can, it seems, account for the relevant sense in which my reasons must suit me. They must suit me in that they must be grounded in the desires and preferences that I in particular ought to have, which may be different from the desires and preferences that others ought to have. For instance, whereas I ought to prefer my child's faring well to your child's faring well, it seems that you ought to prefer your child's faring well to my child's faring well. And neither of us should find this alienating in the way I find my penchant for violent sports alienating, because we can both see reasons why we should have such a preference, as we each have certain

---

[35] Even if they reflect the values that I actually have, they don't reflect the values that I would have if I were substantively rational. Thus, even if I don't find them alienating as I actually am, I would find them alienating if I were substantively rational.

[36] I'm substantively rational if and only if I have every attitude that I'm rationally required to have and only those attitudes that I am rationally permitted to have.

reason-grounding relations with our own child that we lack with respect to the other's child.[37]

3.4 The Motivation Constraint

Subjectivists also claim that their theory supposedly best accounts for the following further constraint on what can count as a reason.

> **The Motivation Constraint:** For any fact F, any subject S, and any act available to them φ, F is a reason (that is, an unqualified reason) for S to φ only if the recognition of F would motivate S to φ in the appropriate circumstances.

But, as with the non-alienation constraint, we need to interpret the phrase "in the appropriate circumstances." On what we may call *the internalist interpretation*, the appropriate circumstances are those in which the subject has no false beliefs, has all the relevant true beliefs, and has deliberated in a procedurally rational way. And deliberating in a procedurally rational way involves using one's imagination to add elements to and to subtract elements from one's initial set of motivations, but it doesn't require one to end up having or lacking any particular motivations. For it requires only that the set of one's motivations and beliefs be jointly coherent.

On *the externalist interpretation*, by contrast, the appropriate circumstances are those in which the subject has no false beliefs, has all the relevant true beliefs, and is substantively rational. And to be substantively rational one must have all the motivations one is rationally required to have and no motivations that one is rationally prohibited from having. To illustrate the difference between these two interpretations, imagine that I have no desire to avoid the destruction of the world but a strong desire to avoid the scratching of my finger. That is, imagine that I don't care if everyone and everything including myself ceases to exist but I do care whether my finger gets scratched. And imagine that I have no false beliefs and have all the relevant true beliefs. Thus I know that I will cease to exist if the world is destroyed and that I will not have the many pleasant experiences that I would otherwise have if I were to cease to exist. And I know that the scratching of my finger will hurt very little and result in no permanent damage or discomfort.

In this case, it could be that my recognizing that I would lose out on a lot of pleasure if the world were destroyed fails to motivate me to opt for the scratching of my finger over the destruction of the world. For it's entirely possible for

---

[37] Note that it's the special relations that come from parenting a child, and not the biological relations that come from spawning a child, that are reason-providing.

me to have no false beliefs, all the relevant true beliefs, and to deliberate in a procedurally rational way and yet end up with no desire to avoid losing out on a lot of pleasure. It may be that all I care about is avoiding immediate pain. By contrast, on the externalist interpretation, knowing the relevant facts will, if I respond appropriately to the reasons that they provide, result in my having a preference for the scratching of my finger over the destruction of the world, which in turn will motivate me to opt for the former over the latter. Thus, on the internalist interpretation of the motivation constraint, I have no reason to choose the scratching of my finger over the destruction of the world. But, on the externalist interpretation, I do as long as we assume that the fact that I would be much better off if my finger were scratched than if the world were destroyed gives me decisive reason to prefer the former to the latter. And that's precisely what the desire objectivist holds. So again we see that desire objectivism can accommodate the relevant constraint provided we interpret it correctly.[38]

3.5 Summing Up

We started this section noting that, intuitively, moral facts (such as the fact that torturing innocents results in people suffering in ways they don't deserve to suffer) seem to be unqualified reasons that are relevant to how we just plain ought to live and not just to how we morally ought to live. Of course we saw that Foot offered an argument against this intuitive view, but we found it wanting because it relied on subjectivism, which we also found wanting. So, absent there being some other more compelling argument against this intuitive view, we should accept that moral reasons are unqualified reasons. What's more, we should accept that certain nonmoral reasons (e.g., self-interested reasons) are also unqualified reasons. Given this, we now need to know how these two different types of unqualified reasons combine and compete to determine what we're morally required to do as well as to determine what we're required to do, all things considered. In the next section, I try to answer these questions.

4 The Normative Significance of Moral Reasons and the Moral Significance of Nonmoral Reasons

In this section, I am concerned with a proper subset of the acts that we ought to perform: those that we're required to perform. More specifically, I am concerned with what role moral reasons play in determining what we're norma-tively/unqualifiedly/rationally required to do – that is, what we're required to

---

[38] Admittedly, there is still much debate about internalism and externalism, and I haven't had space here to fully explore all the nuances. For those interested in these nuances, a good place to start is with Finlay and Schroeder (2017).

do, all things considered. I argue that moral reasons are not normatively overriding, and so we're not always normatively required to do what we have most moral reason to do. I am also concerned with moral requirements. And I argue that moral reasons are not morally overriding, and so we're not always morally required to do what we have most moral reason to do.

4.1 Are Moral Reasons Normatively Overriding?

Let me start by explaining what, in general, I mean when I say that one type of reason (say, moral reasons) is overriding with respect to a given normative domain.

> **Overridingness Defined:** For any subject S, any two acts available to them φ and ψ, and any two normative domains D_1 and D_2 (where D_2 may or may not be identical to D_1), to say that D_1 reasons are D_2-ly overriding is to say that, if S has more D_1 reason to φ than to ψ, then S is not D_2-ly permitted to ψ. And thus, if S has most D_1 reason to φ, then S is D_2-ly required to φ.

Thus to hold that moral reasons are normatively overriding is to accept the following thesis.

> **The Normatively Overriding Thesis:** For any subject S and any two acts available to them φ and ψ, if S has more moral reason to φ than to ψ, then S is not normatively permitted to ψ. And thus, if S has most moral reason to φ, then S is normatively required to φ.

Note that any thesis to the effect that reasons of a certain type (that is, D_1 reasons) are overriding must be indexed to a given domain (say, D_2). And thus we must distinguish the *normatively overriding thesis* – the thesis that moral reasons are normatively overriding (where "D_1" stands for "moral" and "D_2" stands for "normative") – from the *morally overriding thesis* – the thesis that moral reasons are morally overriding (where "D_1" and "D_2" both stand for "moral"). More formally, this latter thesis is as follows.

> **The Morally Overriding Thesis:** For any subject S and any two acts available to them φ and ψ, if S has more moral reason to φ than to ψ, then S is not morally permitted to ψ. And thus, if S has most moral reason to φ, then S is morally required to φ.

The normatively overriding thesis and the morally overriding thesis are different theses. The normatively overriding thesis says that moral reasons trump nonmoral reasons with respect to what one is *normatively* required to do. By contrast, the morally overriding thesis says that moral reasons trump nonmoral reasons with respect to what one is *morally* required to do. In this subsection, I am concerned with the normatively overriding thesis and, in the next, I am concerned with the morally overriding thesis.

If the normatively overriding thesis were true, then it would always be normatively impermissible to refrain from doing what one has most moral reason to do, even when what one has most moral reason to do is supported by only the most trivial of moral reasons and opposed by the weightiest of nonmoral reasons. This is implausible, for it seems that in many instances we have sufficient reason, all things considered, to act contrary to what we have most moral reason to do. For instance, it seems that, in *The Trivial Promise*, I have sufficient, if not decisive reason, to break my promise to meet with the student to discuss their exam grade from the past semester given that this is the only way for me to take advantage of a golden opportunity to fulfill my lifelong dream of sailing around the world. It seems that taking advantage of this opportunity is not what I have most moral reason to do, and yet it does seem to be what I have most reason to do, all things considered. For it seems that the relatively trivial moral reason that I have to keep this promise fails to trump, normatively speaking, the weighty nonmoral reason that I have to take advantage of this once-in-a-lifetime opportunity.

Of course one might counter by suggesting that I have a moral reason to fulfill my lifelong dream such that what I have most moral reason to do in *The Trivial Promise* is to break my promise. But if that were true, we would expect it to be morally bad for me to keep my promise. But that doesn't seem right. If anything, it seems morally noble of me to make such an extreme personal sacrifice for the sake of both fulfilling my promise and letting some more-deserving other get the free trip. So although it may be foolish and imprudent for me to keep my promise in these circumstances, it doesn't seem to be at all morally bad or unchoiceworthy. I wouldn't be morally faulted for keeping my promise. Thus this is a case in which it seems that it's normatively permissible for me to fail to do what I have most moral reason to do. And so we should reject the normatively overriding thesis.

4.2 Are Moral Reasons Morally Overriding?

Recall that the morally overriding thesis holds that even if moral reasons don't trump nonmoral reasons with respect to what we're *normatively* required to do, they trump nonmoral reasons with respect to what we're *morally* required to do. If the morally overriding thesis were true, then it would always be morally wrong to refrain from doing what one has most moral reason to do, even if what one has most moral reason to do is supported by only the most trivial of moral reasons and opposed by the weightiest of nonmoral reasons. But, as *The Trivial Promise* seems to show, it is sometimes not only normatively permissible but also morally permissible for a subject to refrain from doing what they have most moral reason to do. For, in this case, it seems that it is both morally and normatively permissible for me to refrain from keeping my promise even though this is what I have most moral reason to do.

So far all I've done in arguing against the normatively overriding thesis and the morally overriding thesis is to present one case, *The Trivial Promise*, in which it seems both morally and normatively permissible for a subject to refrain from doing what they have most moral reason to do. But, in what follows, I provide a more systematic argument against both theses. I argue that the degree of moral justifying strength that a nonmoral reason has (such as the nonmoral reason that I have to sign up for the free trip) exceeds its degree of moral requiring strength and that this is what accounts for why we are often morally permitted to do either what we have most moral reason to do or what these nonmoral reasons support our doing instead. To illustrate, it seems that, in *The Trivial Promise*, the nonmoral reason that I have to sign up for the free trip morally justifies my breaking my promise, and it does so without morally requiring me to sign up for the free trip instead. Thus I have the moral option of either keeping my promise or breaking it so as to sign up for the free trip. And keeping it seems morally supererogatory – that is, above and beyond the call of moral duty.

Of course that was all rather quick, but next I go through the argument more methodically, starting with definitions of both the moral justifying strength of a reason and the moral requiring strength of a reason.[39]

Moral Requiring Strength: For any two of a subject's reasons R_1 and R_2, R_1 has more moral requiring strength than R_2 if and only if both

(i) R_1 would make it morally impermissible to do anything that R_2 would make it morally impermissible to do, and

(ii) R_1 would make it morally impermissible do some things that R_2 would not make it morally impermissible to do.

Moral Justifying Strength: For any two of a subject's reasons R_1 and R_2, R_1 has more moral justifying strength than R_2 if and only if both

(i) R_1 would make it morally permissible to do anything that R_2 would make it morally permissible to do, and

(ii) R_1 would make it morally permissible do some things that R_2 would not make it morally permissible to do.

To illustrate these criteria for moral requiring strength, consider that, on commonsense morality, the moral reason that one has to refrain from killing

---

[39] These are adapted from Joshua Gert's (2003, pp. 15–16) criteria for rational requiring strength and rational justifying strength.

an innocent person has more moral requiring strength than the moral reason that one has to prevent an innocent person from dying. This is true in virtue of the following two facts: (i) If it would be immoral to do something – for instance, to stand still rather than move about – because that would entail failing to prevent an innocent person's death, then it would also be immoral to do that same thing if it would entail killing an innocent person.[40] (ii) Even though it would be morally permissible to let an innocent person die in order to save one's daughter (as where both are drowning and one has only enough time to save one of the two), it would not be morally permissible to kill an innocent person in order to save one's daughter (as where one's daughter needs that person's heart transplanted into her).

To illustrate these criteria for moral justifying strength, consider that, on commonsense morality, the moral reason that one has to save three lives has more moral justifying strength than the moral reason one has to save one life. This is true in virtue of the following two facts: (i) If it would be morally permissible to do something that would otherwise be immoral – for example, to break a promise to meet with a student – in order to save a life, then it would also be permissible to do the same in order to save three lives. (ii) Even though it would not be morally permissible to fail to save two lives in order to save just one (assuming that everything else is equal and thus that there is no reason that favors saving the one as opposed to the two), it would be morally permissible to fail to save two lives in order to save three.

Having clarified these two notions, I can now state the thesis that I use to argue against both the normatively overriding thesis and the morally overriding thesis. The thesis holds that the degree of moral justifying strength of a nonmoral reason exceeds the degree of its moral requiring strength. It goes as follows.

The More-Justifying-Strength Thesis: Every nonmoral reason is such that the degree of its moral justifying strength (which is greater than zero) exceeds the degree of its moral requiring strength (which is zero).[41] Thus nonmoral reasons can and sometimes do prevent moral reasons, even those with

---

[40] Imagine that, in standing completely still, you would intentionally be allowing the dust to settle on a very sensitive trigger mechanism that, when triggered by the settling dust, blows up the innocent person. This example is inspired by a similar one from Bennett (1995, pp. 97–98).

[41] To illustrate, imagine that the degree of each type of strength can range from zero to infinity, where zero units equals no degree of strength at all. Thus a reason to φ with, say, five units of moral justifying strength would make it permissible to φ even if all the reasons to refrain from φ-ing had a combined total of five units of morally requiring strength. So this thesis says that nonmoral reasons (e.g., the fact that that I would benefit from φ-ing) have more than zero units of moral justifying strength but zero units of moral requiring strength. And since more than zero exceeds zero, the degree of its moral justifying strength exceeds the degree of its moral requiring strength.

considerable moral requiring strength, from generating moral requirements, and they do so without generating a moral requirement to do what they (these nonmoral reasons) favor our doing instead.[42]

Again, to illustrate, the nonmoral reason that I have in *The Trivial Promise* to break my promise (that I must do so in order to get the free trip) morally justifies my breaking my promise despite the fact that the moral reason that I have to keep my promise has considerable moral requiring strength. What's more, it does so without generating a moral requirement to break my promise because the nonmoral reason that I have to break my promise has no moral requiring strength.

If we accept the more-justifying-strength thesis, we should reject both the normatively overriding thesis and the morally overriding thesis. We should reject the morally overriding thesis because the more-justifying-strength thesis implies to the contrary that nonmoral reasons can morally justify acting contrary to what there is most moral reason to do such that we're not always morally required to do what we have most moral reason to do. And if we're *morally* justified in acting contrary to what there is most moral reason to do, then we should think that we're also, contrary to the normatively overriding thesis, *normatively* justified in acting contrary to what there is most reason to do. For it would be implausible to suppose that I could be morally but not normatively justified in failing to do what I have most moral reason to do. After all, if I'm morally justified in failing to do what I have most moral reason to do, this must be in virtue of the nonmoral reasons that I have for doing something else instead. And it would be strange to think that these nonmoral reasons could morally justify my acting contrary to what I have most moral reason to do if they can't even normatively justify my acting contrary to what I have most moral reason to do. So if we accept the more-justifying-strength thesis, we should reject both the normatively overriding thesis and the morally overriding thesis.

But why should we accept the more-justifying-strength thesis? I believe that there are at least two reasons. First, as I argue in Section 4.3, we need the more-justifying-strength thesis to account for many typical instances of what are known as *agent-centered options*. Second, as I argue in Section 4.4, we need the more-justifying-strength thesis to account for many typical instances of *supererogatory acts*.[43]

---

[42] Recall that I'm assuming that moral reasons are also unqualified reasons – that is, are reasons that combine and compete with other unqualified reasons to determine what one just plain ought to do. And I'm also assuming that these nonmoral reasons are unqualified reasons as well.

[43] The following arguments for the more-justifying-strength thesis are adapted from my 2011 (chap. 5).

4.3 Moral Reasons and Agent-Centered Options

The sorts of moral options that I am concerned with are known as *agent-centered options*. An agent-centered option is a moral option either to act so as to make things better overall but worse for oneself (or others) or to act so as to make things better for oneself (or others) but worse overall. Thus there are two types of agent-centered options: *agent-favoring options* and *agent-sacrificing options*. An agent-favoring option is a moral option either to act so as to make things better overall but worse for oneself or to act so as to make things better for oneself but worse overall. For instance, the moral option either to donate my tax refund to charity or to spend it on a trip to Las Vegas for myself is an agent-favoring option. And an agent-sacrificing option is a moral option either to act so as to make things better overall but worse for others or to act so as to make things better for others but worse overall. For instance, the option to use my last dose of painkillers to alleviate someone else's mild pain rather than my own somewhat more severe pain is an agent-sacrificing option. Whereas agent-favoring options permit agents to give their own interests more weight than they have from the impersonal perspective, agent-sacrificing options permit agents to give their own interests less weight than they have from the impersonal perspective.

Now, the following is a typical instance of an agent-centered option (more specifically, an agent-favoring option): an agent has a certain sum of money that they can use to secure either a considerable benefit for themself or a far more considerable net benefit for various needy, distant strangers. Suppose, for instance, that they must choose to use the money that they have saved either to place a down payment on a new home or to help various needy, distant strangers by donating it to an effective charity such as Oxfam.

In this and many other typical instances of agent-favoring options, the following four claims hold:

(C1) The agent has the choice to act either self-interestedly or altruistically – that is, the agent has the choice either to promote their own self-interest or to sacrifice their self-interest for the sake of doing more to promote the interests of others.

(C2) It is morally permissible for the agent to act self-interestedly.

(C3) It is also morally permissible for the agent to act altruistically.

(C4) The reason that the agent has to act altruistically is what I call a moral requiring reason – a moral reason that has sufficient moral requiring strength to generate, absent its requiring force being defeated, a moral requirement to perform the act that it favors.

That claims C1–C3 must hold is, I take it, incontrovertible, as each just follows from the definition of an "agent-favoring option" given earlier. C4, however, probably needs some defense.

To see that the reason that the agent has to act altruistically is, in many typical instances, a moral requiring reason, consider the following two cases.

> *Costly Donation*: Fiona is accessing her savings account via the Internet and is about to transfer the entire balance to her escrow company so as to place the necessary down payment on her new home. She must do this if she is to purchase her new home, and she can do this simply by clicking on the TRANSFER button. However, there is an alternative. By clicking instead on the DONATE button, her savings will be transferred not to her escrow company, but to Oxfam – a charity. Let us suppose, then, that by clicking on the DONATE button she will be providing various needy, distant strangers in the Third World with some considerable, indeed potentially lifesaving, benefit.

Those who accept that there is an agent-centered option in such a case believe that, given the tremendous sacrifice involved, Fiona is not morally required to click on the DONATE button. But it seems that they should also accept that the fact that her doing so would produce such a considerable benefit for these distant, needy strangers constitutes a reason of considerable moral requiring strength to click on the DONATE button. Indeed, but for the costs involved, it seems that this reason would generate a moral requirement to click on the DONATE button.

To see this, consider a variant on this case.

> *Costless Donation*: Fiona can transfer the money to her escrow company by clicking on either the TRANSFER button or the DONATE button. In this case, the money that would be donated to Oxfam if Fiona clicks on the DONATE button is not hers, but that of a very rich woman who has agreed to donate an equivalent sum of her own money if and only if Fiona clicks on the DONATE button. Again, in either case, Fiona's money will be transferred to her escrow company, ensuring the purchase of her new home. It is just that by clicking on the DONATE button as opposed to the TRANSFER button, she also ensures that various needy strangers receive a considerable benefit.

In this case, Fiona is morally required to click on the DONATE button, for there is no good reason why she should not do so. By clicking on the DONATE button, she can purchase her new home while also providing an even more considerable net benefit for a number of others, and she can do so at no cost to herself or anyone else, for assume that if Fiona does not click on the DONATE button, the sum of money that the rich woman would have otherwise donated to Oxfam will instead be burned, benefiting no one. (If one thinks that beneficence is only required when the would-be beneficiaries are below a certain threshold of well-being, assume that the various needy, distant strangers that will be helped by Fiona's clicking on the DONATE button are below this threshold.)

Given that we think that the reason that Fiona has to click on the DONATE button gives rise to a moral requirement in the absence of any fact or reason that defeats its favoring force, we must conclude that it is a moral requiring reason. Now, the only relevant difference between this case and the original one is how costly it is for Fiona to help the strangers. But it is implausible to suppose that Fiona's reason to help the strangers, or its favoring force, is attenuated as the cost of her doing so increases. Neither is it plausible to suppose that its favoring force is nullified when the cost reaches a certain threshold. To illustrate, consider that if we were to gradually increase the cost of clicking on the DONATE button from no cost at all, to ten cents, to twenty cents, to thirty cents, and so on, there wouldn't be less and less to be said in favor of Fiona's helping the strangers. And there certainly wouldn't be any point at which helping those strangers no longer counted in favor of clicking on that button at all. At least, that is not what the phenomenology of the case tells us, for it feels like a case in which one reason is outweighed by another, not like a case in which one reason is attenuated or nullified by some other reason or fact. If it were the latter, then once the cost was high enough, Fiona should cease to feel any pull toward clicking on the DONATE button. But even when the cost is extremely high, the fact that clicking on the DONATE button would help these others continues to count in favor of Fiona's doing so, and with the same force as before. And there is nothing particularly special about this case. So we should conclude that, in many typical instances in which the agent has an agent-centered option, C4 is true.

Of course some moral theorists who endorse agent-centered options could object that although they are committed to certain moral principles, they are not committed to there being any moral reasons, let alone to there being a moral requiring reason to act altruistically in such cases. They might therefore deny that they are committed to C4. But their moral principles commit them to certain moral reasons, for moral principles entail that certain facts have moral requiring strength. For instance, if one accepts the principle of utility (i.e., that agents are required to maximize aggregate utility), then one is thereby committed to there being a moral requiring reason to promote utility. The principle of utility entails that the fact that some act would promote utility is a moral requiring reason to perform that act. Likewise, anyone who accepts a moral principle that entails that agents are obligated to provide needy others with a significant benefit whenever their doing so would be costless both to themselves and to others is thereby committed to there being a moral requiring reason to act altruistically in such instances.

So one of the assumptions that I am making is that some such moral principle is true. If this assumption were false, then Fiona would not, in *Costless Donation*, be obligated to click on the DONATE button. And if that were right, then I would be wrong in saying that those who wish to accommodate many typical agent-centered options are committed to C4. I doubt, though, that my assumption is false. In any case, I assume in what follows that some such moral principle is true and that therefore anyone who wishes to accommodate many typical agent-centered options must accept C4.

Given C4, we must ask: what prevents the moral requiring reason that the agent has to act altruistically from generating a moral requirement to act altruistically? Clearly, it must be the reason that the agent has to act self-interestedly, as this is the only countervailing consideration, and we must cite some countervailing consideration, since, given C4, we are to assume that the moral reason that the agent has to act altruistically would generate a moral requirement to act altruistically absent something that defeats its favoring force. We must also assume that this reason to act self-interestedly must have at least as much moral justifying strength as the reason that the agent has to act altruistically has moral requiring strength – otherwise, it would not be able to prevent the reason that the agent has to act altruistically from generating a requirement to act altruistically. Last, we must assume that this reason to act self-interestedly must have less moral requiring strength than moral justifying strength, for otherwise we would end up with a moral requirement to act self-interestedly instead of a moral option to act either altruistically or self-interestedly. This is Shelly Kagan's worry. He says:

> If, in some particular case, the balance of morally relevant reasons did not favor promoting the overall good [i.e., acting altruistically] but favored instead promoting the agent's own interests [i.e., acting self-interestedly] – then it seems that these reasons would still go on to generate a moral requirement. Admittedly, the agent would not be morally required to promote the overall good, but she would be morally required to promote her interests. Yet . . . what we were looking for was a defense of a moral option, according to which the agent would still be morally permitted (although not required) to do the act with the best results overall. (1994, pp. 338–339)

The solution, as a number of philosophers have pointed out, lies with the fact that the morally relevant reasons that favor acting self-interestedly as opposed to altruistically are nonmoral reasons. If such nonmoral reasons can prevent the moral reason that the agent has to act altruistically from generating a moral requirement, then what we end up with is a moral option rather than a moral requirement to act self-interestedly, for nonmoral reasons, by definition, lack any moral requiring strength. Kagan overlooks this possible solution to his worry because he assumes that the only sorts of reasons that could prevent a moral reason from generating a moral requirement are other moral reasons. He says, "since we are concerned with what is required by morality, the relevant reasons – whether decisive or not – must be moral ones" (1989, p. 66). But Kagan's inference is unwarranted; we should not just assume that nonmoral reasons are irrelevant with regard to what is required by morality. As I argued earlier, nonmoral reasons can be morally relevant facts.

Fortunately for the defender of agent-centered options, it is quite plausible to suppose that the fact that performing some act would further one's self-interest is not itself a moral reason to perform it and thus is not a reason of any moral requiring strength. For there is nothing, morally speaking, that counts in favor of one's promoting one's own self-interest per se. This is not to say that one never has a moral reason to do what will further one's self-interest; one often does, as when doing one's moral duty coincides with promoting one's self-interest. And one may even have a moral duty to ensure that one flourishes and consequently to ensure that one lives happily. But one doesn't seem to have a moral duty to maximize one's happiness or self-interest. So my claim is only that the mere fact that performing some act would further one's self-interest does not itself constitute a moral reason to perform that act.[44]

Consider, for instance, that the fact that I would benefit from drinking a Coke in that it would give me some pleasure doesn't, morally speaking, count in favor of my doing so. If I had the opportunity to get some pleasure by drinking a Coke and chose not to, I could rightly be called foolish or imprudent if I had no good reason not to, but I could not rightly be called immoral – or so it seems.[45] Neither would it be supererogatory for me to change my mind and then get some pleasure by drinking a Coke. And note that promoting one's self-interest in the process of doing what's minimally required doesn't amount to going above and beyond the call of moral duty. Suppose, for instance, that I'm required to save a child drowning in a shallow pond. Promoting my self-interest in the process (by, say, alerting the news media so that I might receive some reward) would not by itself constitute going above and beyond the call of moral duty.

Of course some might object that there are duties to the self (e.g., duties to develop one's talents, to respect one's own dignity, and to ensure that one

---

[44] Thus, on my view, I'm morally permitted to use my last dose of painkillers to alleviate someone else's mild pain rather than my own somewhat more severe pain. Nevertheless, if I have a *pro tanto* moral duty to ensure that I flourish, then it would be wrong for me to sacrifice my life merely to save someone from a mild burn. Chris Tucker (Manuscript) has argued that it would be wrong for me to make such a sacrifice.

[45] Admittedly, the utilitarian believes that I can rightly be called immoral. But this is just one of several areas in which the utilitarian is committed to thinking that things are not as they seem.

flourishes), and that such duties show that there is a moral reason to promote one's self-interest. But the idea that there are certain duties to the self is compatible with the thought that there is no moral reason per se to promote one's self-interest. To illustrate, take the duty to develop one's talents. It seems that this duty derives not from some duty to promote one's self-interest (that is, one's well-being), but from some duty to make use of certain valuable "gifts," and this explains why we are not morally obligated to develop every talent that would be of potential benefit to ourselves. Take, for instance, the ability to walk on one's hands over great distances. This is not the sort of talent that one is morally obligated to develop. Of course one might benefit from developing such a talent, as where one wishes to make it into *The Guinness Book of World Records*. But even so, one would not be morally required, but only normatively required, to develop this talent. Consider also that it would have been wrong for Mozart to have wasted his unique musical talents even if he would have been just as well off (self-interestedly speaking) being a mason instead of a musician. It seems, then, that the wrongness of wasting such great gifts lies with its wastefulness and not with its effects on the individual's self-interest. So we can admit that people are required to make use of certain valuable "gifts" (and thus have certain self-regarding duties), but we should not infer from this that the fact that some act would promote one's self-interest constitutes a moral reason for performing it. That is, we should admit that there is sometimes a moral reason to do that which will promote one's self-interest, but deny that the reason one has to promote one's self-interest is itself a moral reason.

Of course there is no denying that, on some moral theories, such as act-utilitarianism, the reason one has to promote one's self-interest (i.e., to promote one's own utility) is itself a moral reason. But part of the reason why utilitarianism is so counterintuitive is that it implausibly holds that the reason one has to promote one's self-interest is a moral reason. Because of this, the utilitarian must claim that it's immoral for me to refrain from drinking a Coke if this will be best for me and worse for no one. And the utilitarian must claim that it's immoral for me not to alert the media when I'm going to rescue someone if this would promote my self-interest by a greater amount than it would demote the interests of others. In any case, if we want to account for our intuitions in cases like these, we must hold that the reason we have to promote our self-interest is a nonmoral reason and that this nonmoral reason morally justifies our not performing altruistic acts without morally requiring us to perform self-interested acts instead. We should conclude, then, that if we want to accommodate many typical instances of agent-centered options, we must accept:

(C5) The reason that the agent has to act self-interestedly is a nonmoral reason.[46]

What's more, we must accept:

(C6) This nonmoral reason that the agent has to act self-interestedly has sufficient moral justifying strength to prevent the moral reason that they have to act altruistically from generating a moral requirement to act altruistically, and yet it has no moral requiring strength and so doesn't generate a moral requirement to act self-interestedly.

Unless both C5 and C6 are true, there is no way that C1–C4 could all be true. If, contrary to C5, the reason to act self-interestedly was a moral reason, then, as Kagan worries, we'll get either a moral requirement to act self-interestedly (if this moral reason to act self-interestedly outweighs the moral reason to act altruistically) or a moral requirement to act altruistically (if the moral reason to act altruistically outweighs this moral reason to act self-interestedly), when what we were looking for was a moral option to do either.[47] Thus this would contradict either C2 or C3.

And it won't do to deny C6 either, because if we deny that nonmoral reasons have moral justifying strength, then the self-interested reason that the agent has to perform the self-interested option would be powerless to prevent the moral requiring reason they have to perform the altruistic option from generating a moral requirement, for, according to C5, the self-interested reason they have to perform the self-interested option is a nonmoral reason. Clearly, if nonmoral reasons have no moral justifying strength, then they are powerless to prevent moral requiring reasons from generating moral requirements. And, given C4, we must assume that the agent has a moral requiring reason to perform the altruistic option – one that will generate a moral requirement absent its requiring force being defeated. But the only countervailing consideration in this instance

---

[46] We're to assume that Fiona needs neither this money nor this opportunity to put a down payment on a house in order to flourish and live happily.

[47] Admittedly, there are two other possibilities. One possibility is that the reason to act self-interestedly and the reason to act altruistically just exactly balance out. But it seems to me that C2 and C3 would both hold even if we were to slightly up the stakes either for Fiona or for those who would benefit from her donation, thereby ensuring that these two reasons don't exactly balance out. So, this can't be the solution. Another possibility is that the moral favoring force of what we're now taking to be a moral reason to act self-interestedly has no moral requiring force but only a kind of moral enticing force. And in that case, it couldn't generate a moral requirement to act self-interestedly. But even if it has no moral requiring force, the presence of such a moral reason would imply that there is something morally bad or unchoiceworthy about her sacrificing her longer self interest for the sake of promoting the greater interests of others, and this is nearly as implausible as supposing that she's morally prohibited from making such a sacrifice. So I don't think this could be the solution either.

is the reason the agent has to perform the self-interested option, and, as we have just established, this nonmoral reason is, assuming the falsity of C6, incapable of preventing the moral reason the agent has to perform the altruistic option from generating a moral requirement to do so. So we must accept C6 to account for C2.

Thus, in order to accept all of C1–C4, we must accept both C5 and C6. And since we must accept all of C1–C4 if we want to accommodate many typical instances of agent-centered options, it follows that, if we want to accommodate many typical instances of agent-centered options, we must accept both C5 and C6. What's more, we need to accept the more-justifying-strength thesis in general and not just C6, because the thought is not just that this specific nonmoral reason mentioned in C6 behaves in this way, but that all nonmoral reasons behave in this way.

In the next section, I approach the same issue from a different angle, showing that, if we want to accommodate many typical instances of supererogatory acts, we must accept the more-justifying-strength thesis. Thus I believe that insofar as we want to accept our commonsense moral views (views that imply that we have various typical instances of agent-centered options and supererogatory acts), we must accept the more-justifying-strength thesis.

4.4 Moral Reasons and Supererogatory Acts

The word "supererogatory" is the technical term that philosophers use to refer to the concept that the following colloquial expressions refer to: "doing more than one has to," "going the extra mile," and "going above and beyond the call of duty." Thus an act is morally supererogatory (hereafter, simply "supereroga-tory") if and only if, in performing it, the agent exceeds the minimum that's morally required. Given this understanding, there are at least two necessary conditions for an act's being supererogatory:

Two Necessary Conditions: For any subject S and any act available to them φ, S's φ-ing is supererogatory only if there exists some available alternative, ψ, such that:

(NC$_1$) S is both morally permitted to φ and morally permitted to ψ, and

(NC$_2$) S has more moral reason to φ than to ψ.

NC$_1$ is necessary because if there were no permissible alternative, the act would be obligatory. And, in that case, it wouldn't go *beyond* the call of duty; it would just be part of one's duty – that is, part of what one's minimally required to do.

And NC_2 is necessary because the act wouldn't go *above* the call of duty if it were not more morally choiceworthy than what's minimally required of the subject. Now, some might deny that NC_2 states a necessary condition for an act's being supererogatory, claiming instead that an act is supererogatory if and only if it is both morally optional (NC_1) and morally praiseworthy. While I do not (at least, not here) want to deny (or assert) that a supererogatory act must be morally praiseworthy, I do want to defend NC_2.

Consider, then, that an act can be both morally optional and morally praiseworthy without going above and beyond the call of duty. To illustrate, consider the following case, which I borrow from Paul McNamara.

> *Soldier on Point*: A soldier is on point this evening. It is her turn to guard the camp. As a general policy and by mutual agreement of everyone in the camp, the soldier on point has the choice of holding either a first or a second position, the first being slightly better with respect to protecting the camp and the second being slightly safer for the soldier on point. This evening the enemy launches a massive assault on the camp in an attempt to overrun it. Despite the grave danger involved and the temptation to run and hide, our soldier faithfully holds the second position, losing her life in the process but providing those back at the camp with sufficient time to prepare and launch a successful counter assault. (This is adapted from his 2011, p. 220.)

In holding the second position, our soldier does the least that they can permissibly do – the minimum required. Doing anything less than holding the second position (such as running and hiding) would have been impermissible. But even though our soldier did not go above and beyond the call of duty (as our soldier would have had they held the first position), the soldier's actions are praiseworthy. As McNamara points out, "to stay on point (in either position) in the face of a high chance of death for the sake of others, knowing the advantages of running and having a much better chance of survival, is surely praiseworthy" (2011, p. 220).

Thus our soldier did something that was both morally optional (given that the soldier had the option of holding the first position instead) and morally praiseworthy (given that it is praiseworthy to face such a high chance of death for the sake of others even when this is obligatory). But the soldier's act wasn't supererogatory. For in performing this act the soldier didn't go above and beyond the call of duty. Had our soldier held the more personally dangerous but more altruistic first position, the soldier would have. But our soldier didn't. The soldier did only the minimum required.

A further reason to accept NC_2 as a necessary condition is that it nicely accounts for the normative force that supererogatory acts supposedly have. Supererogatory acts are acts that are more morally choiceworthy than their non-supererogatory alternatives. Indeed, the facts that make an act super-erogatory are presumably considerations that, morally speaking, count in favor of performing it as opposed to any of its non-supererogatory alterna-tives. But if, contrary to NC_2, agents do not have more moral reason to perform a supererogatory act than to perform its non-supererogatory alterna-tives, then it is hard to see why there is supposedly something that, morally speaking, counts in favor of their doing so. So we should accept that both NC_1 and NC_2 constitute necessary conditions for an act's being supererogatory.

Once we accept these two necessary conditions, though, supererogation can seem impossible since NC_2 appears to be in tension with NC_1, as James Dreier has explained:

> Morality, we are inclined to think, is a matter of what reasons one has from the moral point of view. When there is a supererogatory act available, it would be better for you to perform it. So surely you have a reason, from the moral point of view, to perform the act. You may have some reason not to perform it, but at least typically you have no reason from the moral point of view [that is, no moral reason] to refrain from it (if you do have such reason, then it will ordinarily be outweighed by the reason you have to perform, because by hypothesis it is better to perform). But now it is hard to see how it could be permissible, from the moral point of view, to refrain from doing something that you have an undefeated reason (from that very point of view) to do. Everything from the moral point of view speaks in favor of your [performing the supererogatory act], and nothing at all speaks against it . . . [In] what sense is it "all right," "permissible," "not wrong" to fail [to do so]? There seems to be no sense at all. Supererogation, according to this way of seeing things, turns out to be impossible. (2004, p. 148)

This is known as the paradox of supererogation, and it stems from the fact that the following three claims are jointly inconsistent:

(C7) For any subject S and any act available to them φ, S's φ-ing is super-erogatory only if there exists some available alternative ψ such that: (NC_1) S is both morally permitted to φ and morally permitted to ψ, and (NC_2) S has more moral reason to φ than to ψ. [From the definition of "supererogatory".]

(C8) For any subject S and any two distinct acts available to them φ and ψ, if S has more moral reason to φ than to ψ, then S is not morally permitted to perform ψ. [From the morally overriding thesis.]

(C9) There are supererogatory acts. [Assumption]

These are jointly inconsistent because, given C8, it follows that, whenever NC_2 is met, NC_1 isn't. And this means that no act can be supererogatory, which contradicts C9. To solve the paradox, the supererogationist (i.e., the person who accepts that there are supererogatory acts as defined in C7) must deny C8. And in doing so, they must explain why the morally undefeated reason that favors performing the supererogatory act fails to generate a moral requirement.

If one wants to deny C8 (i.e., the morally overriding thesis), then one must accept either or both of the following two theses.

The More-Justifying-Strength Thesis: The degree of a nonmoral reason's moral justifying strength (which is greater than zero) exceeds the degree of its moral requiring strength, which is zero.

The No-Requiring-Strength Thesis: Some moral reasons have no moral requiring strength.

There are, then, two possible (and not mutually exclusive) explanations for why the morally undefeated reason that favors performing the supererogatory act fails to generate a moral requirement to so act. One explanation involves appealing to the no-requiring-strength thesis, claiming that the moral reasons for performing the supererogatory alternative have no moral requiring strength and are thus incapable of generating a moral requirement. Call this *the non-requiring-moral-reason explanation*. Another possible explanation, though, involves appealing to the more-justifying-strength thesis, claiming that the relevant nonmoral reasons justify acting contrary to the moral reasons for performing the supererogatory alternative and thereby prevent those moral reasons from generating a moral requirement. Call this *the non-moral-reason explanation*.

Philosophers such as James Dreier and Michael J. Zimmerman overlook the non-moral-reason explanation because they assume that the more-justifying-strength thesis is false.[48] According to them, nonmoral reasons are irrelevant to the determination of an act's moral status, for they overlook the possibility that nonmoral reasons can be morally relevant facts. Hence they assume that the non-requiring-moral-reason explanation is the only possible explanation.

---

[48] That Dreier (2004) rejects the non-moral-reason explanation is clear from the fact that he thinks that an act's moral status is a function of solely moral reasons – see the first sentence in the previously cited quote as well as what he says on page 149 of the same article. Zimmerman, by contrast, is less explicit, but he does say that if there being more moral reason to perform the supererogatory alternative is essential to supererogation, then any theory wishing to accommodate supererogation will have to declare that there are two sets of moral reasons, deontic and non-deontic reasons (or what I am calling *moral reasons with* and *moral reasons without* moral requiring strength) – see Zimmerman (1993, pp. 375–376).

In an effort to spell out how exactly the non-requiring-moral-reason explanation might go, Dreier speculates that there might be two moral points of view, one being the point of view of justice and the other being the point of view of beneficence. Dreier further speculates that reasons stemming from justice have considerable moral requiring strength, but that reasons stemming from beneficence have no moral requiring strength. According to Dreier, supererogatory acts are more beneficent, but not more just, than their non-supererogatory alternatives. So although agents have more moral reason to perform a supererogatory act than to perform any of its non-supererogatory alternatives, they are not morally required to do so, for the relevant reasons (i.e., reasons of beneficence) have no moral requiring strength – they're non-requiring moral reasons.

The problem with Dreier's particular suggestion, and with the general suggestion that the non-requiring-moral-reason explanation is the only possible explanation, is that they both rest on the mistaken assumption that the reasons that make a supererogatory alternative morally superior to its non-supererogatory alternatives are always moral reasons of no moral requiring strength. To the contrary, it seems that in many typical instances of supererogation the moral reasons that favor performing the supererogatory alternative over its non-supererogatory alternatives are moral requiring reasons.

To illustrate, recall *Costly Donation*, where Fiona must choose between acting so as to secure a considerable benefit for herself by transferring the money from her savings account to her escrow account and acting so as to secure a more considerable benefit for various needy, distant strangers by instead donating those funds to Oxfam. In that case, her forfeiting the chance to buy a new home and instead donating her savings to Oxfam is supererogatory. Given that Dreier and Zimmerman insist on the no-moral-requiring-strength explanation, they must deny that the moral reason that favors Fiona's donating the money to Oxfam as opposed to transferring it to her escrow company is a moral requiring reason. If it were, then her donating the money to Oxfam would, on their view, be obligatory, not supererogatory, because, on their view, whatever nonmoral reason she has to purchase a new home would be powerless to prevent the moral requiring reason that she has to donate the money to Oxfam from giving rise to a moral requirement to so act. But, as we have already seen, the moral reason that favors her donating the money to Oxfam is a moral requiring reason, for, absent countervailing considerations, Fiona is morally required to donate the money to Oxfam. And there are many other similar cases in which the moral reason that the agent has to perform some beneficent and supererogatory act is a moral requiring one. So if we are to account for many typical instances of supererogation, we are going to have to accept the nonmoral-reason explanation, thereby accepting, contrary to Dreier and others, that nonmoral reasons, and not just moral reasons, are relevant to the determination of an act's deontic status. That is, we must accept the more-justifying-strength thesis.

4.5 An Objection to This Account

I've argued that we should accept the more-justifying-strength thesis in part because we must do so in order to account for many typical agent-centered options. Now, my account is inspired by Michael Slote's similar account (see his 1991). Consequently, mine is subject to many of the same objections to which his is subject. And one of these is the following objection from Shelly Kagan.

> Slote is arguing, in effect, that whenever the agent has a moral option, then from the rational point of view the reasons the agent has for favoring her own interests outweigh the reasons that support promoting the greater good [that is, support acting altruistically] ... But if this is so, then what if anything prevents these reasons from grounding a rational requirement to favor her interests in each such case? (1991, p. 927)

If the answer is that nothing would, then this would seem to be an unacceptable result both for Slote and myself, for it would mean that in such cases "it would be rationally forbidden – irrational – to choose to do the morally preferable act [i.e., the supererogatory act]" (Kagan 1991, pp. 927–928). This would seem unacceptable for at least two reasons. First, it seems unacceptable to suppose that, whenever there is a moral option, performing the morally preferable (and thus supererogatory) option is necessarily rationally/normatively forbidden. Second, it seems unacceptable to suppose that, whenever there is a moral option, there is a rational requirement (or, in other words, a normative requirement) to perform the self-interested option, for what we want to account for is the intuition that there is both a moral and a rational (i.e., normative) option to act either altruistically or self-interestedly.

Nevertheless, Kagan's objection is, as stated, a bit too quick, for, contrary to what Kagan says, Slote and I need not claim that, from the rational point of view (that is, the point of view of all reasons), the nonmoral reason the agent has to act self-interestedly *outweighs* the moral reason the agent has to act altruistically. For we can instead claim that these two opposing reasons exactly balance out. And if they do, then we can plausibly claim that the fact that there is just as much overall reason to act self-interestedly as to act altruistically accounts for the lack of a moral requirement to act altruistically. Moreover, since there is just as much reason, all things considered, to perform the one as the other, there will be a rational option to do either. And thus we can account for the intuition that there is both a moral and a rational option to act either altruistically or self-interestedly.

As convenient as this might be, Kagan finds it implausible to suppose that in all the typical instances of agent-centered options the altruistic reasons and the self-interested reasons exactly balance out. As Kagan suggests, it seems that such ties would be too rare to account for the wide range of options we take there to be. So Kagan's objection amounts to the following worry. If the reasons that favor the two alternatives are not exactly balanced out, then one or the other alternative will be rationally (i.e., normatively) required even if not morally required. What's more, the reasons that favor the two alternatives will only very rarely exactly balance out. Therefore, this strategy for defending agent-centered options involves trading, in most instances, a moral requirement for a rational requirement, when what we were looking for was both a moral and a rational option to act either altruistically or self-interestedly.

It is important to realize, though, that the problem of accounting for rational options given the seeming implausibility of supposing that the relevant reasons always exactly balance out is a difficult philosophical problem that befalls anyone interested in accounting for what Joseph Raz calls "the basic belief," and he calls it this because it seems so clearly correct that we should give it "credence unless it can be shown to be incoherent or inconsistent with some of our rightly entrenched views" (2000, p. 100). It is as follows.

> **The Basic Belief:** The basic belief is the deeply entrenched commonsensical belief that in many typical choice situations, the relevant reasons do not require performing one particular act-type, but instead permit performing any of a variety of different act-types, such as gardening, watching TV, volunteering for Oxfam, reading the newspaper, or working on a book.[49]

It seems, for instance, that I could now, in accordance with reason, perform any of these very different act-types. But how are we to account for this? It

---

[49] As Raz states things, the basic belief is the belief "that most of the time people have a variety of options such that it would accord with reason for them to choose any one of them and it would not be against reason to avoid any of them" (2000, p. 100). But interpreted literally, this seems too weak to capture the belief that Raz has in mind. For I take it that Raz doesn't mean to be discussing the belief that we always have a variety of options that would accord with reason given that there are always countless permissible ways of performing a required act-type. For instance, suppose that reason requires that I push a certain button with my right index finger. Even so, I'll have a variety of options that would accord with reason given that there are countless permissible ways for me to push that button with my right index finger. I can do so as quickly as possible or not as quickly as possible. I can do so while singing the national anthem or while keeping quiet. I can do so while tapping my foot or while not tapping my foot. And so on and so forth. I take it, then, that Raz has in mind the belief that there is often a variety of different act-types that we could perform that would all accord with reason, such as watching TV, painting the fence, volunteering for Oxfam, reading the newspaper, or working on a book.

seems that there could be such rational options only if there were exactly equal reason to perform each of the optional alternatives, and yet it is hard to believe that such is the case. For instance, it is hard to believe that I have just as much reason to watch TV as either to volunteer for Oxfam or to work on this book. After all, volunteering for Oxfam seems vastly superior to watching TV in terms of the amount of impersonal good that it would do, and working on this book seems vastly superior to watching TV in terms of the amount of good it would do me – assume that I am not at this moment too tired to work productively on the book. Moreover, the fact that, in many of these choice situations, the relevant alternatives remain rationally optional even after there has been a small increase in the number and/or the strength of the reasons that favor just one of the alternatives seems to show that their rationally optional status could not have been due, in the first place, to a perfect balance of reasons (Gert 2008, p. 14). For instance, it seems that it would still be rationally permissible for me to continue to work on this book even if there were a slight increase in the strength and/or number of reasons that favor just one of the other options, as where, say, Oxfam institutes a new policy of giving each volunteer a delicious cookie. So the puzzle is to explain how, in most choice situations, there could be so many rationally optional alternatives given that it is seemingly implausible to suppose that there is exactly equal reason to perform each one of them.

What this all means is that the problem of accounting for rational options is not any more serious for the defender of agent-centered options than it is for anyone else who accepts the basic belief. And if the problem is not specific to the aforementioned account of agent-centered options, then it is no objection to this account that it encounters the same problem that anyone wishing to account for rational options faces. What's more, I have argued elsewhere that this problem can be solved and in a way that's conducive to the sort of account that Slote and I want to give.[50]

In this section, I've argued that moral reasons are neither normatively nor morally overriding. I've argued that the degree of a nonmoral reason's moral justifying strength exceeds the degree of its moral requiring strength. And this enables nonmoral reasons to prevent moral reasons, even those with consider-able moral requiring strength, from generating moral requirements, and to do so without generating a moral requirement to do what they favor. I've argued that we must accept this view in order to accommodate many typical instances of agent-centered options and supererogatory acts.

---

[50] See my 2011 (chap. 6) and my 2019a (chap. 6). I argue that, despite Kagan's skepticism, there is indeed exactly equal reason to perform each of the relevant alternatives. But see Gert (2018) for some worries about my solution to accommodating the basic belief and for some alternative solutions.

Now, this view implies that moral reasons are not inherently more important than nonmoral reasons when it comes to determining how we ought to live. For, in determining how we ought to live, we will, on this view, need to consider not only our moral reasons but also our nonmoral reasons. But even if *moral reasons* are not especially normatively important, it may be that *moral requirements* are. Indeed, I believe that they are. For, as I argue in the next section, moral requirements are supremely normatively important in that we must abide by them if we are to live as we just plain ought to live.

5 The Normative Significance of Moral Requirements

If we accept that nonmoral reasons are morally relevant reasons in that they have sufficient moral justifying strength to prevent the moral requiring strength of moral reasons from generating a moral requirement to do what there is most moral reason to do (say, φ), then we need to ask when do these nonmoral reasons to do something other than φ (say, ψ) prevent the moral reasons that favor φ-ing from generating a moral requirement to φ? There are just three possibilities. Possibility 1: They do so even when they and any moral reasons that also favor ψ-ing have *less* combined normative weight than do all the reasons (moral and nonmoral) that favor φ-ing. On this possibility, we will sometimes be morally permitted to ψ even though we have not only more moral reason but also more reason, all things considered, to φ than to ψ. Possibility 2: They do so only when they and any moral reasons that also favor ψ-ing, have *at least as much* combined normative weight as do all the reasons (moral and nonmoral) that favor φ-ing. On this possibility, we will be morally permitted to ψ only when we have at least as much reason, all things considered, to ψ as to φ. Possibility 3: They do so only when they and any moral reasons that also favor ψ-ing have *more* combined normative weight than do all the reasons (moral and nonmoral) that favor φ-ing. On this possibility, we will be morally permitted to ψ only when we have more reason, all things considered, to ψ than to φ.

It seems to me that Possibility 2 is the most plausible. For it seems that if we don't do what we have most moral reason to do (viz., φ) and instead ψ, we need some sort of excuse or justification for not φ-ing. And it seems that we'll have adequate justification for not doing what we have most moral reason to do (viz., φ) if we have at least as much reason, all things considered, to ψ as to φ. So, it seems that we must accept Possibility 2. And this means we should accept the following.

Moral Rationalism (MR): For any subject S and any act available to them φ, if S is morally required to φ, then S is normatively required to φ – that is, S has decisive (and thus most) reason, all things considered, to φ.

Moral rationalism (MR) offers the most plausible explanation for why nonmoral reasons have moral justifying strength: if I can't be morally obligated to do what I don't have decisive reason to do, then, given that all reasons (including nonmoral reasons) are relevant to what I have decisive reason to do, they'll also be relevant to what I'm morally required to do. But besides explaining this important phenomenon, I think that MR is just good common-sense. There are several reasons for this. First, MR accounts for the fact that moral requirements serve as a rational/normative constraint on how and to what extent we may pursue our own personal aims and projects. For "morality's felt role as a constraint on the pursuit of those aims would be undermined if it were OK – not morally OK, but OK from this more encompassing point of view [of normativity in general] – to ignore moral injunctions in favor of those projects" (Stroud 1998, p. 176). In other words, MR accounts for why it's normatively impermissible for us to ignore moral injunctions so as to pursue our own personal aims and projects: it's because we're always normatively required to act as morality requires us to act. And thus "moral requirements place rational [i.e., normative] constraints on our actions. If someone has a moral obligation to act in a particular way then we do not think that she is free to choose how to act. Rather, we think that she has most reason [all things considered] to do what is morally required" (Archer 2014, p. 107). Second, MR accounts for the fact that a commitment to do as morality requires strikes us, not as a rationally arbitrary personal choice or preference, but as the rationally required response to the interests and claims of others. In choosing to act as I'm morally required to act rather than as I'm selfishly disposed to act, I seem to be choosing rationally rather than just plunking for acting altruistically rather than selfishly. That is, it feels like I'm responding appropriately to the relative normative weights of my own concerns as well as those of others.[51] And, third, MR explains why figuring out that we're morally required to act in a certain way seems sufficient for figuring out what we ought to do, all things considered. For instance, it seems that if I've settled that I'm morally required to refrain from eating meat, then this settles for me the question of whether I ought to refrain from eating meat. And thus we are inclined to take someone's response "That's what I was morally

---

[51] Admittedly, not everyone shares this intuition. For instance, Gert thinks that there are powerful people who act normatively/unqualifiedly permissibly when they act morally wrongly for the benefit of themselves. He says, "my pre-theoretical intuition is that these immoral people have plenty of reason to want to behave in the [immoral] ways in which they do, and these reasons are not overridden by the reasons they have to behave in [moral] ways" (2014, p. 218). Now, I agree that they have plenty of self-interested reasons to act immorally and that these reasons are not *overridden* by the moral reasons they have for doing something else, but I believe that they must be *outweighed* by the moral reasons for doing something else; for otherwise we would not think it immoral for them to act self-interestedly just as we don't think it immoral for me to act self-interestedly in *The Trivial Promise*.

required to do" as sufficient normative justification for how they acted, even if what they did was culturally, aesthetically, or self-interestedly suboptimal. As Archer puts it, "moral requirements provide a rational justification for action. If we accept that an act is morally required then there does not seem to be any need to give a further rational justification for performing that act" (2014, p. 108). And, fourth, MR explains why "showing that an act was in line with what an agent had most reason to do seems sufficient to show that the act was not morally wrong. It would be odd for someone to claim that an act was in line with what she had most reason to do but also morally impermissible" (Archer 2014, p. 109). After all, on MR, the reason for this is plain: "moral requirements are always in line with what there is most reason to do. As a result, showing that an act is not what an agent has most reason to do is sufficient to show that it is not morally required" (Archer 2014, p. 109).

For all these reasons, MR seems to be built into our ordinary conception of morality. But I don't settle for this alone. I provide a deeper explanation for MR in what follows, one that has to do both with the fact that "morally wrong" just means "morally blameworthy absent some suitable excuse (such as ignorance or the inability to do otherwise)" and with the fact that no one can be morally blameworthy for doing something morally bad if that's something they had sufficient reason, all things considered, to do – and this holds even if they had no other suitable excuse or justification for doing so.[52] Thus, if I step on your toe and you object, demanding that I account for my action, it seems that I will succeed in doing just that if I can demonstrate to you that I had sufficient (and thus good) reason for stepping on your toe.

Now, there are two ways I might try to argue for moral rationalism. I could argue that the correct substantive accounts of both moral requirements and normative (or what others call "rational") requirements are such that the former is a proper subset of the latter, thus ensuring that MR holds. Alternatively, I could try to establish MR independently of any such substantive accounts. And this is the route that I take.

But, even having chosen this route, I still need to choose between two further possibilities. On one possibility, I would argue for the normatively overriding thesis – the view that moral reasons normatively override all other types of reasons.[53] For if the normatively overriding thesis were true, MR would follow.

---

[52] As I see it, whether you have an *excuse* for doing something morally bad bears on whether you're morally responsible for having done so. By contrast, whether you have a *justification* for doing something morally bad bears on whether you were morally wrong in having done so.

[53] Stephen Darwall, however, suggests the following possible defense of the normatively overriding thesis: "Can moral reasons actually reduce or eliminate the weight of a countervailing reason? It surely seems that they can. Consider, for example, the pleasure a torturer might take in seeing her victim squirm. In such a case, the wrongness of torture or of taking pleasure in

But I do not take this tack, as I've already argued against the normatively overriding thesis. On the other possibility, the one that I favor, I try to establish MR on the basis of certain relevant conceptual connections – specifically, a conceptual connection both between responsibly violating a moral requirement and being blameworthy and between having sufficient reason to perform an act and not being blameworthy for performing that act. But before I can clearly state my argument, I need to clarify some relevant terminology.[54]

First, to say that a subject has *decisive reason*, all things considered, to φ is to say that their reasons are such as to make them rationally/normatively required to φ, and to say that they have *sufficient reason*, all things considered, to φ is to say that their reasons to φ are such as to make them rationally/normatively permitted to φ.[55] Thus, a subject has decisive reason, all things considered, to φ if and only if they do not have sufficient reason, all things considered, to refrain from φ-ing. And I use "a subject, S, has decisive reason to φ" and "S has sufficient reason to φ" as shorthand for "S has decisive reason, all things considered, to φ" and "S has sufficient reason, all things considered, to φ," respectively.

Second, to say that a subject has sufficient reason to φ is to say that there is at least one act-token that is an instance of them φ-ing that they have sufficient reason to perform. And to say that they have decisive reason to φ is to say that they have decisive reason to perform an instance of the φ-type.

Third, to say that a subject *freely* φ-ed is to say that they meet the control condition (sometimes called the freedom condition) for being morally responsible for having φ-ed, such that they had the relevant sort of control over whether they were to φ – the sort of control that's required for their being appropriately praised or blamed for having φ-ed.

Fourth, to say that a subject *attributively* φ-ed is to say that they meet the ownership condition for being responsible for having φ-ed, such that they had the relevant sort of ownership over their having φ-ed – the sort of ownership that's required for their being appropriately praised or blamed for having φ-ed. In other words, in φ-ing, they sufficiently expressed their values, character, and/ or judgments about reasons such that they count as being morally responsible for having φ-ed.

---

others' pain seems not only to outweigh any reason provided by the pleasure; it seems to 'silence' it" (2006b, p. 287). But I'm not convinced that there is any countervailing reason in this case – that is, I'm not convinced that sadists have any reason to do what will give them sadistic pleasure.

[54] This is based off the argument that I provided in my 2011 (chap. 2).

[55] With this and the other definitions, I leave implicit that we could replace "φ" with "refrain from φ-ing" throughout.

Fifth, to say that a subject *knowledgeably* φs is to say that they meet the knowledge condition (sometimes called the epistemic condition) for being morally responsible for having φ-ed, such that they had the relevant sort of knowledge concerning the nature and effects of their φ-ing – the sort of knowledge that's required for their being appropriately praised or blamed for having φ-ed.

Sixth, to say that a subject is *blameworthy* for having φ-ed is to say both that it is appropriate for them to be blamed for having φ-ed and thus for them to feel guilty for having φ-ed and for others to feel indignation – and perhaps also resentment – toward them for having φ-ed.[56] And here I use "appropriate" in the sense of being apt, fitting, or correct and thus in the same sense that fear is the appropriate response to something that one perceives as posing a danger to oneself. In this sense, it can be appropriate to blame oneself or someone else even though having this attitude (and/or expressing it) would be instrumentally bad.

Seventh and last, when I say that a subject is *morally required* to φ, I mean this in the objective (or fact-relative) sense – the sense in which I'm required to unplug a toaster that's about to start a fire even if I have no evidence suggesting that leaving the toaster plugged in poses a danger.

With these terms defined, I can now state my argument as follows:

(P1) For any subject S and any option of theirs φ, if S is morally required to φ, then S would be blameworthy for freely, attributively, and knowledgeably refraining from φ-ing.[57] [A conceptual truth[58]]

(P2) For any subject S and any option of theirs φ, if S would be blameworthy for freely, attributively, and knowledgeably refraining from φ-ing, then S does not have sufficient reason to refrain from φ-ing. [Assumption]

(Inf₁) Thus, for any subject S and any option of theirs φ, if S is morally required to φ, then S does not have sufficient reason to refrain from φ-ing.[59] [From P1 and P2]

---

[56] For more on this and on the nature of blame, see Portmore (Forthcoming).

[57] If you think that the set of conditions that are necessary and sufficient for being morally responsible for φ-ing is something other than the conjunction of the control condition, the ownership condition, and the knowledge condition, then feel free to make that substitution here and elsewhere. Essentially the claim here is just that, if S is morally required to φ, then S would be blameworthy for morally responsibly refraining from φ-ing.

[58] I think that this is just as much a conceptual truth as "If S is a bachelor, then S doesn't have a spouse" is.

[59] "P*x*" indicates a premise and "Inf*x*" indicates the product of an inference (that is, a conclusion).

(P3) For any subject S and any option of theirs φ, if S does not have sufficient reason to refrain from φ-ing, then S has decisive reason to φ. [From the definitions of "sufficient reason" and "decisive reason"]

(Inf₂) Therefore, for any subject S and any option of theirs φ, if S is morally required to φ, then S has decisive reason to φ – and this just is MR. [From Inf₁ and P3]

The argument is deductively valid. P1 is intuitively plausible. Indeed, it expresses the common assumption that there is a conceptual connection between wrongdoing and blameworthiness.[60] Although there may not be an essential connection between wrongdoing and blameworthiness per se, there is, it seems, an essential connection between blameworthiness and responsibly doing wrong – that is, between blameworthiness and freely, attributively, and knowledgeably doing wrong. P2 is also intuitively plausible.[61] In any case, there is, I think, a sound argument for it, which is based on assumptions that are even more intuitively plausible than itself. But before I present that argument, let me rebuff some putative counterexamples to P2.

Consider the following example. Suppose that Arthur, a white supremacist, sneaks up behind an unsuspecting black man named Bert and clubs him over the head, knocking him unconscious. Now, it's good that he did so, for Bert was just about to kill his ex-girlfriend Carla, who's completely innocent. So, as it turns out, Arthur saves Carla's life, as any less violent or injurious act would have been insufficient to prevent Bert from killing Carla. And let's assume that Arthur knew what Bert was about to do, but that this wasn't what motivated him. What motivated him was solely the desire to hurt a black person.

In this case, it seems that Arthur had sufficient reason to club Bert over the head, and yet clearly he is blameworthy. But this is no clear counterexample to P2. For although it is clear that Arthur is blameworthy, it is far from clear that Arthur is blameworthy for clubbing Bert over the head, which is what would need to be true for this to constitute a counterexample to P2. So I think that we can rightly blame Arthur for his vicious motive, for his malevolent intent, and for his racist attitudes.[62] We can even rightly blame him both for acting out of

---

[60] See, for instance, Darwall (2006a), Gibbard (1990), Mill (1991), and Skorupski (1999).

[61] Proponents include Darwall (2006b) and Wedgwood (2013). Even some of those who deny moral rationalism admit that P2 is quite intuitive. See, for instance, David Sobel, who explicitly denies moral rationalism (see 2007a) and yet claims that it "seems quite intuitive that earnestly blaming a person for [φ]-ing entails the view that the agent all things considered ought not to have [φ] ●d" (2007a, p. 133).

[62] For a defense of the view that we can be morally responsible for our motives, intentions, and other attitudes, see both my 2019a (chaps. 2 and 3) and my 2019b.

hatred and malice and for being willing to club Bert over the head even if there had been no good reason for him to do so. But I do not think that we can rightly blame him for clubbing Bert over the head, as this is exactly what he should have done. Later in life, when Arthur finally comes to realize the error of his ways, what he should come to regret and feel guilty about is the fact that he was a racist who acted out of hatred and malice. Arthur should not, however, regret having clubbed Bert over the head, neither should he feel guilty for having done so, for this is what he had sufficient (indeed, decisive) reason to do. To accept blame for having φ-ed, one must judge that one should not have φ-ed. But although he should neither have wished Bert harm nor acted out of hatred or malice, he should have clubbed him over the head, as this was necessary to save Carla's life.

So, although it is clear that Arthur is blameworthy for something, it is not clear that he is blameworthy for freely, attributively, and knowledgeably doing anything that he had sufficient reason to do. Thus the proponent of P2 can reasonably claim that there is no φ such that Arthur had sufficient reason to φ and yet is blameworthy for freely, attributively, and knowledgeably φ-ing. If, on one hand, we let "φ" stand for "clubbing Bert over the head," then although it is clear that Arthur had sufficient reason to φ, it is not so clear that he is blameworthy for freely, attributively, and knowledgeably φ-ing. And if, on the other hand, we let "φ" stand for, say, "acting out of malice," then although it is clear that Arthur is blameworthy for freely, attributively, and knowledgeably φ-ing, it is not so clear that he had sufficient reason to φ. So I do not see this is as a clear counterexample to P2. Having cleared this up, let me now explain why we should accept P2.

The thought underlying P2 is that agents are blameworthy only for freely, attributively, and knowledgeably doing what they lack sufficient reason to do. One way to bring out the intuitive plausibility of this claim is to point to the tension there is in blaming someone for acting in a certain way while acknowledging that they had sufficient reason to act in that way. Stephen Darwall puts the point thusly:

> It seems incoherent . . . to blame while allowing that the wrong action, although recommended against by some reasons, was nonetheless the sensible thing to do, all things considered . . . Part of what one does in blaming is simply to say that the person shouldn't have done what he did, other reasons to the contrary notwithstanding. After all, if someone can show that he had good and sufficient reasons for acting as he did, it would seem that he has accounted for himself and defeated any claim that he is to blame for anything. Accepting blame involves an acknowledgment of this proposition also. To feel guilt is, in part, to feel that one shouldn't have done what one did. (2006b, p. 292)

Another way to bring out the intuitive plausibility of P2 is to point to the tension there is in holding someone morally responsible for their actions on account of their having the capacity to respond appropriately to the relevant reasons and then blaming them for responding appropriately to the relevant reasons by doing what they had sufficient reason to do. Let me explain. It seems that an agent can be blameworthy for their actions only if they are morally responsible for them and that they can be morally responsible for them only if they have the relevant sort of control over their actions. What's more, it is plausible to suppose that they have the relevant sort of control over their actions only if they have the capacity to respond appropriately to the relevant reasons – that is, the capacity both to recognize what the relevant reasons are and to react appropriately to them, being moved by them in accordance with their associated normative weights. Indeed, it is this capacity for responding appropriately to the relevant reasons, which sane adult humans typically possess and which young children, primitive animals, and the criminally insane typically lack, that distinguishes those who can be held accountable for their actions from those who cannot.

   Given that an agent can be morally responsible (and, thus, blameworthy) only if they have the capacity to respond appropriately to the relevant reasons, it is important to note that, in flawlessly exercising this capacity, they could be led to perform any act that they have sufficient reason to perform. But if an agent is morally responsible for their actions and thus potentially blameworthy for their actions in virtue of their having the capacity to respond appropriately to the relevant reasons, then how can we rightly blame them for acting as they are led to act in flawlessly exercising this very capacity? Surely it cannot be that the very capacity that opens the door to the possibility of their being blameworthy is the one that leads them to walk through that door, performing a blameworthy act. And yet this is exactly what we would be allowing if we held that agents can be blameworthy for performing acts that they have sufficient reason to perform, for it is their capacity to respond appropriately to the relevant reasons that opens the door to their being blameworthy in the first place – a capacity that, when exercised flawlessly, leads them to perform acts that they have sufficient reason to perform.

   To put the point in slightly different terms, it seems that appropriate blame cannot be unjust, and yet it would be unjust to hold an agent responsible on the condition that they have the capacity to be guided by sound practical reasoning and then blame them for acting as they might very well be led to act if they are guided by sound practical reasoning. And since an agent can be led to perform any act that they have sufficient reason to perform when guided by sound practical reasoning, it seems inappropriate to blame them for freely, attributively, and knowledgeably doing what they have sufficient reason to do, as this would be unjust.

Consider an analogy. It seems that appropriate instructional penalties cannot be unjust, and yet it would be unjust to penalize a student for their writing errors on the condition that they have the capacity for errorless writing and then penalize them for writing in a way that they might very well be led to write in flawlessly exercising this capacity. To illustrate, imagine that I hold only those students who have the capacity for errorless writing responsible for their writing errors, penalizing their writing errors. By contrast, I don't penalize students who lack this capacity. Further suppose that those with the capacity for errorless writing are often led in flawlessly exercising this capacity to rewrite a sentence such as "Jeff likes hiking and to swim" as "Jeff likes hiking and swimming" – thus replacing a sentence with a nonparallel structure with one with a parallel structure. But, now, imagine that, for some strange reason, I deduct points from all students (regardless of their capacities) who employ parallel structures in their writing. Thus I penalize a student who writes "Jeff likes hiking and to swim" only if they have the capacity for errorless writing. But I penalize every student (regardless of their capacities) who writes something like "Jeff likes hiking and swimming." This seems unjust. For those who lack the capacity for errorless writing don't get penalized when they fail to rewrite a sentence such as "Jeff likes hiking and to swim," and yet those who have this capacity are penalized when they rewrite "Jeff likes hiking and to swim" as "Jeff likes hiking and swimming," which is precisely what they may be led to do in flawlessly exercising this capacity. Thus they have the right to complain that if other students get excused for not rewriting a sentence like "Jeff likes hiking and to swim" given that they lack the capacity for errorless writing, then they shouldn't be penalized for rewriting it as they may be led to by the very capacity that opens them up to being penalized for failing to rewrite it.

More formally, my argument for P2 is as follows.

(PI) S would be blameworthy for freely, attributively, and knowledgeably refraining from φ-ing only if S has the relevant sort of control over whether they refrain from φ-ing. [From the definition of "freely"]

(PII) S has the relevant sort of control over whether they refrain from φ-ing only if S has the capacity to respond appropriately to the relevant reasons. [Assumption[63]]

---

[63] I defend this assumption in chapters 2 and 3 of my 2019a.

(Inf$_I$) Thus S would be blameworthy for freely, attributively, and knowledge-ably refraining from φ-ing only if S has the capacity to respond appropriately to the relevant reasons. [From PI and PII]

(PIII) If S has sufficient reason to refrain from φ-ing, then, in flawlessly exercising their capacity to respond appropriately to the relevant reasons, S could be led to freely, attributively, and knowledgeably refrain from φ-ing. [A conceptual truth]

(PIV) If S would be blameworthy for freely, attributively, and knowledgeably refraining from φ-ing only if S has the capacity to respond appropriately to the relevant reasons, then S cannot be blameworthy for freely, attributively, and knowledgeably refraining from φ-ing when, in flawlessly exercising this capacity, S could be led to freely, attributively, and knowledgeably refrain from φ-ing. [Assumption]

(Inf$_{II}$) Thus S would not be blameworthy for freely, attributively, and knowledgeably refraining from φ-ing if S has sufficient reason to refrain from φ-ing. [From Inf$_I$–PIV]

(Inf$_{III}$) Therefore S would be blameworthy for freely, attributively, and knowledgeably φ-ing only if S does not have sufficient reason to φ – and this just is P2. [From Inf$_{II}$]

In considering this argument, it will be helpful to have a specific example in mind. So consider a revised version of *The Trivial Promise*. In this version, we replace the offer of a free trip around the world on a luxury sailing yacht with a less appealing alternative such that I have only exactly as much reason, all things considered, to drive down to the city to accept this offer as to show up to my meeting as promised. And assume that I have considerably less reason to do anything besides these two. Thus assume that I have sufficient reason to do either of these two, but insufficient reason to do anything else. Furthermore, assume that I am flawless in exercising my capacity to respond appropriately to reasons, such that I always do what I have decisive reason to do, only do what I have sufficient reason to do, and choose arbitrarily which of two acts to perform (by, say, tossing a coin) if and only if I have sufficient and equivalent reason to do either. And let's assume that, having sufficient and equivalent reason to do either, I choose arbitrarily to drive down to the city to accept the offer. That is, assume that I first designate heads to driving down to the city to accept the offer and designate tails to showing up to the meeting as promised and then toss a coin, which lands heads. As a result, I decide to drive down to the city, missing my meeting with the student.

Of course, being flawless in how I exercise my capacity to respond appropriately to my reasons, I would have kept my promise and met with the student had there been decisive reason to do so. For instance, I would have kept my promise had my moral reason for doing so been a bit stronger, as where, say, the student's scholarship was at stake. Likewise, I would have kept my promise had my self-interested reason for driving down to the city been a bit weaker, as where, say, the offer had been a bit less enticing. And had there been a third option that I had decisive reason to do (e.g., saving some drowning child), I would have done that instead. But, as it was, none of these were true. As it was, I had sufficient reason to drive down to the city and thereby break my promise to meet with the student. And that is what I did, having flawlessly exercised my capacity for sound practical reasoning.

Given my flawless exercise of my capacity for sound practical reasoning, how can I be faulted for breaking my promise? It seems unjust and thus inappropriate to hold me morally responsible for what I've done in virtue of my having the capacity to respond appropriately to my reasons and then blame me for acting as I was led to act in virtue of responding appropriately to my reasons. Indeed, it seems that even the student whom I stood up should admit that, had they been in my situation and perfectly rational, they might also have been led to act as I did. And if so, how can they rightly resent me for acting as they would have acted in such circumstances?

I've argued that moral rationalism can be known *a priori* and thus that we can know that it's true independently of our doing any first-order theorizing about the substance of our requirements.[64] Thus I believe that we know that moral rationalism is true, not because we know both what we're morally required to do and what we're normatively required to do and see that the former is a proper subset of the latter, but because we understand that certain *a priori* necessary connections among moral requirements, normative permissions, and blameworthiness entail moral rationalism. Specifically, I've argued that, as a matter of conceptual necessity, if we're morally required to φ, then we are blameworthy for freely, attributively, and knowledgeably refraining from φ. Yet we can't be blameworthy for freely, attributively, and knowledgeably refraining from φ-ing if this is something we're normatively permitted to refrain from

---

[64] Note that I haven't argued that moral rationalism is analytic in the way that "If X is bachelor, then X is unmarried" is. "Being normatively required to φ" isn't part of the analysis of "being morally required to φ" in the way that "being unmarried" is part of the analysis of "being a bachelor." To be normatively required to φ isn't part of what it means to be morally required to φ. Rather, what it means for φ to be something that one is morally required to do is for φ to be something that one would be blameworthy for refraining from doing absent some suitable excuse.

doing. So we can't be morally required to do what we're normatively permitted to refrain from doing. And therefore moral rationalism is true.[65]

6 Conclusion

I've argued for a commonsense approach to morality and practical reasons. I've argued that, other things being equal, we should accept that things are as they seem. Thus we should accept that there are agent-centered options, that there are supererogatory acts, that moral reasons are unqualified reasons, and that moral requirements are normatively authoritative. This means that there are only two ways to resist my arguments. One way is to resist my account of how things seem. Thus some readers might deny that moral reasons seem to be unqualified reasons or that moral requirements seem to be normatively authoritative. But even the leading critics of these positions accept my account of how things seem. For instance, the leading proponent of subjectivism, David Sobel, concedes that moral reasons *seem* to be unqualified reasons. Besides, I have, in each case, given reasons for accepting my account of how things seem. For instance, I've given four reasons for thinking that the idea that moral requirements are normatively authoritative – that is, moral rationalism – is built into our ordinary conception of morality.

The only other way to resist my arguments is to argue that other things are not equal and that the cost of accepting these seemingly true claims is just too high in terms of our having to reject other things that seem to be true. For instance, some subjectivists (e.g., Sobel) have argued that, although it seems that moral reasons are unqualified reasons, we cannot accept this without failing to adequately explain how our rationally contingent pro-attitudes affect what we have reason to do, which is something that also seems to be true. But, in each case, I've argued that, in fact, there are no significant costs in our accepting these seemingly true claims. For instance, I've argued that we can adequately

---

[65] Dale Dorsey (2015 and 2016) has objected to my argument on the grounds that in assuming P1, I'm begging the question and just presupposing that moral rationalism is true. And, in Dorsey (2016), he claims to provide two arguments that putatively show that "without a prior commitment to moral rationalism, (1) should simply be rejected" (p. 56), where "(1)" stands for what I've labelled here "(P1)." But his first argument, which he calls *the explanation argument*, argues instead that P1 "can only be rendered plausible if we are already committed to" P2 of that same argument (2016, p. 57). And this doesn't show that P1 is question-begging. His second argument, which he calls *the epistemological argument*, argues instead that "if *a priori* [moral] rationalism is true then the fact that extra-moral considerations play a role in determining the extent to which φ-ing is morally justified can be established independently of a first-order inquiry into the content of the moral domain" (2016, p. 64). And this too fails to show that P1 is question-begging. Dorsey does, however, provide an argument against my P2 in his Forthcoming, but I believe that his argument relies on a false account of when blame is appropriate – see my Forthcoming.

explain how our rationally contingent pro-attitudes affect what we have reason to do while accepting that moral reasons are unqualified reasons. Of course not everyone will agree. And so I've tried throughout to highlight where some of these disagreements may lie.[66]

---

[66] For helpful comments on earlier drafts, I thank Alfred Archer, Dale Dorsey, Ben Eggleston, James Fanciullo, Andrew Forcehimes, Dale Miller, Daniel Muñoz, Shyam Nair, David Sobel, Travis Timmerman, and two anonymous reviewers.

References

Archer, A. (2014). "Moral Rationalism without Overridingness." *Ratio* 27: 100–114.

Baggini, J. (2015). "A New Breed of Hardcore Altruists Are Changing the Way We Think about Charity. But Can Generosity Go too Far?" *New Statesman*, <www.newstatesman.com/economics/2015/08/new-breed-hardcore-altruists-are-changing-way-we-think-about-charity-can>.

Bennett, J. (1995). *The Act Itself*. Oxford: Clarendon Press.

Berg, A. (Manuscript). "How and Why to Be Well-Rounded."

Cohen, S. (1999). "Contextualism, Skepticism, and the Structure of Reasons." *Philosophical Perspectives* 13: 57–89.

Copp, D. (1997). "The Ring of Gyges: Overridingness and the Unity of Reason." *Social Philosophy and Policy* 14: 86–106.

Copp, D. (2009). "Toward a Pluralist and Teleological Theory of Normativity." *Philosophical Issues* 19: 21–37.

Dancy, J. (2006a). "Nonnaturalism." In D. Copp, ed., *The Oxford Handbook of Ethical Theory*. New York: Oxford University Press, pp. 122–145.

Dancy, J. (2004). "Enticing Reasons." In R. J. Wallace, P. Pettit, S. Scheffler, and M. Smith, eds., *Reason and Value: Themes from the Moral Philosophy of Joseph Raz*. Oxford: Oxford University Press, pp. 91–118.

Dancy, J. (2006b). "What Do Reasons Do?" In T. Horgan and M. Timmons, eds., *Metaethics after Moore*. Oxford: Oxford University Press, pp. 39–59.

Darwall, S. (2006a). *The Second-Person Standpoint: Morality, Respect, and Accountability*. Cambridge, MA:Harvard University Press.

Darwall, S. (2017). "What Are Moral Reasons?" *Amherst Lecture in Philosophy* 12: 1–24, <www.amherstlecture.org/darwall2017/>.

Darwall, S. (2006b). "Morality and Practical Reason: A Kantian Approach." In D. Copp, ed., *The Oxford Handbook of Ethical Theory*. Oxford: Oxford University Press, pp. 282–320.

Dorsey, D. (2015). "How Not to Argue against Consequentialism." *Philosophy and Phenomenological Research* 90: 20–48.

Dorsey, D. (2016). *The Limits of Moral Authority*. Oxford: Oxford University Press.

Dorsey, D. (Forthcoming). "Respecting the Game: Blame and Practice Failure." *Philosophy and Phenomenological Research*.

Dreier, J. (2004). "Why Ethical Satisficing Makes Sense and Rational Satisficing Doesn't." In M. Byron, ed., *Satisficing and Maximizing*. Cambridge: Cambridge University Press, pp. 131–154.

Finlay, S., and M. Schroeder (2017). "Reasons for Action: Internal vs. External." In E. N. Zalta, ed., *The Stanford Encyclopedia of Philosophy* (Fall 2017 Edition). URL = <https://plato.stanford.edu/archives/fall2017/entries/reasons-internal-external/>.

Foot, P. (1972). "Morality As a System of Hypothetical Imperatives." *Philosophical Review* 81: 305–316.

Forcehimes, A. T., and L. Semrau (2018). "Are There Distinctively Moral Reasons?" *Ethical Theory and Moral Practice* 21: 699–717.

Gert, J. (2003). "Requiring and Justifying: Two Dimensions of Normative Strength." *Erkenntnis* 59: 5–36.

Gert, J. (2008). "Michael Smith and the Rationality of Immoral Action." *Journal of Ethics* 12: 1–23.

Gert, J. (2014). "Perform a Justified Option." *Utilitas* 26: 206–217.

Gert, J. (2018). "Underdetermination by Reasons." In D. Star, ed., *The Oxford Handbook of Reasons and Normativity*. Oxford: Oxford University Press, pp. 443–460.

Gibbard, A. (1990). *Wise Choices, Apt Feelings: A Theory of Normative Judgment*. Cambridge, MA.: Harvard University Press.

Haldane J. (2011). "Is Every Action Morally Significant?" *Philosophy* 86: 375–404.

Hume, D. (1975). [1739]. *A Treatise of Human Nature*, L. A. Selby-Bigge (ed.), 2nd ed. revised by P. H. Nidditch, Oxford: Clarendon Press.

Joyce, R. (2001). *The Myth of Morality*. Cambridge: Cambridge University Press.

Kagan, S. (1989). *The Limits of Morality*. Oxford: Oxford University Press.

Kagan, S. (1991). "Replies to My Critics." *Philosophy and Phenomenological Research* 51: 919–928.

Kagan, S. (1994). "Defending Options." *Ethics* 104: 333–351.

MacAskill, W. (2013). "To Save the World, Don't Get a Job at a Charity; Go Work on Wall Street." *Quartz*, <https://qz.com/57254/to-save-the-world-dont-get-a-job-at-a-charity-go-work-on-wall-street/>.

MacAskill, W. (2015). *Doing Good Better*. New York: Gotham Books.

Markovits, J. (2014). *Moral Reason*. Oxford: Oxford University Press.

McLeod, O. (2001). "Just Plain 'Ought.'" *Journal of Ethics* 5: 269–291.

McNamara, P. (1996). "Making Room for Going Beyond the Call." *Mind* 105: 415–450.

McNamara, P. (2011). "Supererogation, Inside and Out: Toward an Adequate Scheme for Common Sense Morality." In M. Timmons, ed., *Oxford Studies in Normative Ethics, Volume I*. Oxford: Oxford University Press, pp. 202–235.

Mill, J. S. (1991). [1861]. *Utilitarianism*. In J. M. Robson, ed., *Collected Works of John Stuart Mill, Vol. 10*. London: Routledge, pp. 203–259.

Nair, S. (2016). "Conflicting Reasons, Unconflicting 'Oughts.'" *Philosophical Studies* 173: 629–663.

Parfit, D. (1997). "Reasons and Motivation." *Proceedings of the Aristotelian Society*, suppl. 71: 99–130.

Parfit, D. (2011). *On What Matters. Vol. 1.* Oxford: Oxford University Press.

Portmore, D. W. (2011). *Commonsense Consequentialism: Wherein Morality Meets Rationality.* New York: Oxford University Press.

Portmore, D. W. (2019b)." Control, Attitudes, and Accountability." *Oxford Studies in Agency and Responsibility* 6: 7–32.

Portmore, D. W. (2019a). *Opting for the Best: Oughts and Options.* New York: Oxford University Press.

Portmore, D. W. (Forthcoming). "A Comprehensive Account of Blame: Self-Blame, Non-moral Blame, and Blame for the Non-voluntary." In A. Carlsson, ed., *Self-Blame and Moral Responsibility.* Cambridge: Cambridge University Press.

Raz, J. (2000). *Engaging Reason: On the Theory of Value and Action.* Oxford: Oxford University Press.

Sagdahl, M. S. (2014). "The Argument from Nominal–Notable Comparisons, 'Ought All Things Considered,'and Normative Pluralism." *Journal of Ethics* 18: 405–425.

Scanlon, T. M. (1998). *What We Owe to Each Other.* Cambridge, MA.: Belknap Press.

Schroeder, M. (2007). *Slaves of the Passions.* Oxford: Oxford University Press.

Singer, P. (2015). *The Most Good You Can Do.* New Haven, CT: Yale University Press.

Sinnott-Armstrong, W. (1992). "An Argument for Consequentialism." *Philosophical Perspectives* 6: 399–421.

Skorupski, J. (1999). *Ethical Explorations.* Oxford: Oxford University Press.

Slote, M. (1991). "Shelly Kagan's *The Limits of Morality.*" *Philosophy and Phenomenological Research* 51: 915–917.

Sobel, D. (2007a). "Subjectivism and Blame." *Canadian Journal of Philosophy* 33 (Supplement): 149–170.

Sobel, D. (2007b). "The Impotence of the Demandingness Objection." *Philosophers' Imprint* 7: 1–17.

Sobel, D. (2016). *From Valuing to Value: A Defense of Subjectivism.* Oxford: Oxford University Press.

Streumer, B. (2007). "Reasons and Impossibility." *Philosophical Studies* 136: 351–384.

Stroud, S. (1998). "Moral Overridingness and Moral Theory." *Pacific Philosophical Quarterly* 79: 170–189.

Tiffany, E. (2007). "Deflationary Normative Pluralism.".*Canadian Journal of Philosophy* 37: 231–262.

Tucker, C. (Manuscript). "Too Far Beyond the Call of Duty: Moral Rationalism and Weighing Reasons."

Wedgwood, R. (2013). "The Weight of Moral Reasons." In M. Timmons, ed., *Oxford Studies in Normative Ethics, Volume III*. Oxford: Oxford University Press, pp. 35–58.

Worsnip, A. (Forthcoming). "Immorality and Irrationality." *Philosophical Perspectives*.

Zimmerman, M. J. (1993). "Supererogation and Doing the Best One Can." *American Philosophical Quarterly* 30: 373–380.

Cambridge Elements ⹀

Ethics

Ben Eggleston
University of Kansas

Ben Eggleston is a professor of philosophy at the University of Kansas. He is the editor of *John Stuart Mill, Utilitarianism: With Related Remarks from Mill's Other Writings* (Hackett, 2017) and a coeditor of *Moral Theory and Climate Change: Ethical Perspectives on a Warming Planet* (Routledge, 2020), *The Cambridge Companion to Utilitarianism* (Cambridge, 2014), and *John Stuart Mill and the Art of Life* (Oxford, 2011). He is also the author of numerous articles and book chapters on various topics in ethics.

Dale E. Miller
Old Dominion University, Virginia

Dale E. Miller is a professor of philosophy at Old Dominion University. He is the author of *John Stuart Mill: Moral, Social and Political Thought* (Polity, 2010) and a coeditor of *Moral Theory and Climate Change: Ethical Perspectives on a Warming Planet* (Routledge, 2020), *A Companion to Mill* (Blackwell, 2017), *The Cambridge Companion to Utilitarianism* (Cambridge, 2014), *John Stuart Mill and the Art of Life* (Oxford, 2011), and *Morality, Rules, and Consequences: A Critical Reader* (Edinburgh, 2000). He is also the editor in chief of *Utilitas*, and the author of numerous articles and book chapters on various topics in ethics broadly construed.

About the Series
This Elements series provides an extensive overview of major figures, theories, and concepts in the field of ethics. Each entry in the series acquaints students with the main aspects of its topic while articulating the author's distinctive viewpoint in a manner that will interest researchers.

Cambridge Elements ≡

Ethics

Elements in the Series

A full series listing is available at http://www.cambridge.org/EETH

Printed in the United States
by Baker & Taylor Publisher Services